ADVANCED HANDGUN SURVIVAL TACTICS
Second Edition

The Porter Method is for police officers and people with similar firearms training who use a handgun for self-defense.

This book can turn target shooters into tactical shooters and show tactical shooters how to use a handgun or shotgun to stop a knife attack.

Advanced Handgun Survival Tactics

Second Edition
Copyright © 2012, 2013, 2022
All rights reserved—No portion of this book may be reproduced, stored, or transmitted without express permission from the author.

"This publication includes images from CorelDRAW® 9 which are protected by copyright laws of the U.S., Canada and elsewhere. Used under license."

NOTICE

We wrote this for police officers or people with similar firearms training who use a handgun for self-defense. Handguns can cause serious bodily injury or death, and the writers and publisher disclaim any liability because of injury or loss that results from reading this book. The people using the material in this book are responsible for their own safety and for knowing when they need to seek medical, legal, or other professional advice. The writers and the publisher recommend you speak to a doctor and follow the doctor's advice concerning physical or mental limitations, and you seek professional advice if you need more information about any topic in this book. This book is being sold without any warranties, the information in this book is not a substitute for working with a qualified firearms instructor, and this book was written specifically for police and military personnel who have already mastered the skills that are needed to use a firearm safely and with reasonable proficiency.

If possible, do not shoot without eye and ear protection. Prescription glasses might not be reliable for eye protection. If you use a handgun for self-defense, wearing tactical ear protection can make you more combat effective.

This book cannot provide specific information relating to the kind of guns you might use for self-defense. Readers are responsible for knowing how to use and maintain any gun they use.

Unlike a competitive target shooter, a competent tactical shooter needs to have good shooting skills and good tactical skills. You cannot be a competent tactical shooter if you have never practiced hitting a moving target or have never practiced moving and shooting at the same time, and you cannot be a competent tactical shooter if you don't know how to use cover correctly or how to protect yourself against a knife attack. A competent tactical shooter also needs to understand the relationship between tactical anatomy and good shot placement.

DISCLAIMERS

The laws relating to self-defense are different in each state, and what's legal in one state might be illegal in another state. The authors are not attorneys, and this book does not give legal advice. If you need legal advice, please speak with someone qualified to give you the legal advice you need.

Self-defense laws are constantly changing. They can be reinterpreted because of case law. Many of the laws have exceptions, and the instructions that judges give juries can significantly impact how the laws are applied. In some cases, public opinion affects jury decisions more than admissible evidence or laws. Doing something tactically correct that saves your life might not be legally correct and might result in criminal charges or civil lawsuits.

The information in this book is based on personal field experience, scientific and medical studies, statistical data, historical information, logic, facts, and common sense. Readers must weigh the evidence we present and decide if our suggestions satisfy their needs. Whenever possible, we try to justify our reasons for taking a particular position on an issue, but we also realize some of the positions we take in this book will be controversial.

Handguns are dangerous and may cause serious bodily harm or death, and even experts trained to use firearms safely can make serious or fatal mistakes. The information about handgun safety in this book provides some general guidelines, but we wrote this book for people who have already mastered the essential skills they need to use a handgun safely and with reasonable proficiency. The information in this book is for *academic study only*. Regardless of what we recommend in this book, law enforcement officers have a legal obligation to obey the administrative orders issued by their departments.

Reading a book will not help you become a competent tactical shooter unless you practice what you have learned. The information in this book can and has saved lives, but knowledge is not power unless you apply the knowledge. After you learn a tactical technique, you cannot maintain or improve your ability to use the technique without practice. To be a competent tactical shooter, you need to practice critical shooting techniques until you automatically perform them correctly without hesitation. A few of the critical close-quarter-combat shooting skills you need to master are shooting with a target focus instead of a front-sight focus, shooting with both eyes open, shooting with one hand, and shooting while moving.

TABLE OF CONTENTS

DISCLAIMER i

PREFACE 1

DEDICATION 2

BASIC PRINCIPLES 3

WHY WE WROTE THIS BOOK 4
LISTEN TO THE EXPERTS 5

INTRODUCTION 6

POLICE FIREARMS TRAINING 8
    NEW YORK CITY POLICE DEPARTMENT (NYPD) 10

SELF-DEFENSE 11

LEGENDARY GUNFIGHTERS 12
    DUELING AND OLD WEST GUNFIGHTING 12
    MODERN GUNFIGHTERS: USE A TARGET FOCUS 16

SHOT PLACEMENT 18
    HEADSHOT 19
    HEART SHOT 23
    PELVIC SHOT 24
    UNEXPECTED INCAPACITATION 25
    REASONABLE FORCE 25
        ANTERIOR AND POSTERIOR AIM POINTS 26
        LATERAL AIM POINTS AND CENTR OF MASS 27
        BRAINSTEM AND UPPER SPINE AIM POINTS 28
        AVOID TARGET SHOOTER AIM POINTS 29
        SUMMARY 30

DEFENSE AMMUNITION	31
PENETRATION	32
PERMANENT WOUND CAVITY	32
TEMPORARY WOUND CAVITY	32
HANDGUN SAFETY	33
SIX BASIC HANDGUN RULES	33
HANDGUN SHOOTING SKILLS	34
ADVANCED AIMING TECHNIQUES	40
MALFUNCTIONS	41
MULTIPLE TARGETS	42
QUICK DRAW AND HOLSTERS	43
TACTICAL SKILLS	45
PROGRESSIVE LEVELS OF AWARENESS	46
FIGHTING TO WIN	47
DECEPTIONS, DISRUPTIONS, AND DISTRACTIONS	47
AMBUSH	48
ACTS OF DESPERATION	48
REALITY OR MYTH	49
TACTICAL AXIOMS	49
DANGER SIGNES	50
ACTIONS AND REACTIONS	50
LIGHTING	51
MISSES THAT MIGHT COUNT	52
HOW TO BE A HARD TARGET	52
MOBILITY	53
SURRENDERING YOUR GUN	53
RELAXING TOO SOON	54
BUILDING SEARCHES	55
A BASIC ROOM SEARCH	57
HOME SECURITY	58
STREET CONFRONTATIONS	60
INDICATIONS OF DECEPTION	64

TACTICAL TRAINING PROTOCOLS 66
   PRACTICAL SHOOTING 69
   DRY FIRE PRACTICE AND LASER PRACTICE 70
   NON-LETHAL HANDGUNS... 71
   RICOCHET.. 72
   MENTAL PRACTICE... 73
   HANDLING STRESS AND PANIC 74
   NO LIGHT AND LOW-LIGHT PRACTICE 75
   HOLLYWOOD PRODUCTIONS 76
   FIX THE PROBLEM, NOT THE BLAME 77

HOW TO STOP A KNIFE ATTACK 78
   ANATOMY OF A KNIFE ATTACK 85
   IF YOU ANTICIPATE A KNIFE ATTACK................................ 89
      FIGHT THE PERSON, NOT THE KNIFE............................. 89
      NO REAL WINNERS 89
      CHECK YOUR BODY 89
   STOPPING A KNIFE ATTACK WITH A SHOTGUN 90

A TACTICAL TARGET FOR HANDGUNS....................................... 96

COMBAT BIBLIOGRAPHY... 98

ABOUT THE AUTHORS 107

Based on tactical anatomy and forensic science:

When using a handgun, the aim point for a combat-effective heart shot or headshot is a 5-inch circle, and a tactical shooter's goal is to hit anywhere within an aim point as quickly as possible. Taking extra time to aim so you can hit the center of an aim point will increase your risk of getting killed. If you need to cause immediate incapacitation, you need to make a headshot. A center-of-mass shot that misses the heart or the large blood vessels surrounding the heart might not cause any incapacitation. You might win a shooting competition by hitting a 10-inch steel plate, but you won't cause combat-effective incapacitation if you can't hit a 5-inch aim point.

INTRODUCTION

People who have never used and handgun for self-defense often fail to realize that tactical shooting has two parts: tactical skills and shooting skills. Most police officers have better tactical skills than most competitive target shooters, and most competitive target shooters have better shooting skills than most police officers. If you compare the tactical and shooting skills that most police officers have with the tactical and shooting skills that most FBI agents have, it would be obvious that FBI agents have better tactical and shooting skills than most police officers. As Dustin Salomon pointed out in his book Building Shooters, "Most people who carry guns for a living suffer from inadequate entry-level training and inadequate in-service training."

Becoming a competent tactical shooter requires good training and regular practice. Most police officers receive poor firearms training because most states have qualification standards that almost anyone with five days of basic firearms training could easily pass. Federal agencies, such as the FBI and DEA, receive more tactical firearms training and have higher qualification requirements than most police departments.

Just reading this book will not make you a competent tactical shooter, but it may help you separate reality from myth. For example: Hollywood created the quick-draw myth. You seldom won a gunfight in the Old West because of a quick draw. Having a reliable draw is more important than having a fast draw.

In his book The Tactical 1911, Dave Lauck correctly stated that "Shot placement will remain a critical factor in ending any encounter, and a 'failure to stop situation' has occurred with nearly all cartridges, including those reputed to be 'manstoppers.'" To stop someone with one shot, you need to understand tactical anatomy and have good shot placement.

This book, Advanced Handgun Survival Tactics, is right on target. After two tours in Vietnam with the Army's 5th Special Forces (Green Berets), I questioned the quality of the firearm training I received in the police academy…. In Vietnam we learned that the best way to end an enemy threat was to use a headshot, which usually caused immediate incapacitation and was often the only part of the enemy you could target…. This book emphasizes what most combat veterans already know: being a good target shooter does not make you a good tactical shooter.

Herbert L. Brown, Colonel, USAF (Retired)

DEDICATION

We dedicate this book to the law enforcement officers who died in the line of duty because they were poorly trained. Rather than teach the shooting skills and tactical skills that are needed to survive a deadly confrontation, most police departments teach their officers just enough about shooting and tactics to meet minimum state standards. FBI and DEA agents usually have better shooting and tactical skills than the average police officer because their training is better, and FBI and DEA agents the federal agents must meet higher minimum standards. Rather than raise their qualification standards, it appears that many states are lowering their qualification standards and making it nearly impossible for anyone not to qualify.

High-capacity magazines are not a good substitute for good shot placement. According to some recent studies, police officers have a 30% hit rate, which means they hit the person they aim at about 70% of the time. Rather than relying on good marksmanship and good shot place, many of the police officers you see on television seem to rely on a technique called *spray and pray*. In other words, keep shooting until your high-capacity magazine is empty and hope you hit the person who is shooting at you or attacking you with a knife.

When you see a police officer on television jump out from behind a car or tree and then stand in the open while shooting multiple rounds at an active shooter, it is hard to believe their training included tactical skills such as how to use cover or concealment. It makes you wonder about their tactical skills when you see officers confronting someone threatening to kill them with a knife, and they have their guns holstered. A gun in your hand is worth more than two holstered guns.

Reality-based is often used when training First Responders but seldom used when teaching shooting or tactical skills. If you want to improve a police officer's survival skills, you should not teach shooting and tactical skills as two separate topics. You should teach an officer a shooting skill and then show the officer how to combine the shooting skills with appropriate tactical skills. For example, standing in the open and shooting a stationary target might be an excellent way to introduce gun safety and basic marksmanship, but in the real world, when someone is shooting at you, you might need to shoot and move and the same time or you might need to run for cover. In some cases, both you and the shooter might be moving and shooting at the same time.

Since most police departments do not teach tactical anatomy, it's not surprising that most police officers do not understand shot placement. You might be able to qualify by hitting the center of mass most of the time, but you might not stop a knife attack unless you fire a shot that causes immediate incapacitation. Even multiple center-of-mass hits with a .45 caliber bullet might not cause immediate incapacitation, but one well-placed 9mm bullet will cause immediate incapacitation.

BASIC PRINCIPLES

Even though this book is about advanced handgun survival techniques, some of the essential techniques that will save your life are basic techniques. Many of the police officers killed in the line of duty might be alive today if their training stressed the importance of following these basic principles.

John Steinbeck stated, "The final weapon is your brain." Try to maintain 360-degree awareness of your surroundings. Constantly look for potential threats and take appropriate actions to protect yourself if you see a potential threat. It's safer to take your gun out of its holster if you think you might need it and return it to its holster if you don't need it than to have it in your holster when you do need it. For example, if you believe someone might attack you with a knife, your gun should be out of its holster. If someone holding a knife threatens to kill you, your gun should be pointing at the person who is threatening to kill you.

Know what you are aiming at before you shoot. You do not win a deadly confrontation by missing the person you are shooting at, and you might not win if none of your hits cause incapacitation. If someone attacks you with a gun and you fire a shot that stops your adversary's heart, your adversary might be fully functional for 10 to 15 seconds, which is more than enough time to return fire and kill you. If none of your shots cause immediate incapacitation, you might be able to take cover and continue shooting, or if you are very close to your adversary, you might be able to move your adversary's gun away from your body and make a headshot.

Relaxing too soon is a deadly mistake that often gets police officers injured or killed. A deadly confrontation is not over until you eliminate all deadly threats. Do not assume you have disarmed someone until you restrain and search the person. Restraining someone before you do a complete search will make it harder for someone to grab your gun. Until someone is restrained, watch their hands and make it hard for them to watch your hands. Stay alert. Never assume that eliminating one deadly threat has eliminated all deadly threats. This topic will be discussed again.

Use cover whenever possible. If you can safely reach cover, shooting while using cover is safer than shooting without cover. If you are in the open when a deadly threat suddenly appears, it might be safer to move and shoot than run for cover, especially if you already have your gun in your hand. Good police training should include shooting from behind cover. Be aware that some cover might give you good protection, and other cover, such as a car door, might give you limited protection.

WHY WE WROTE THIS BOOK

In *Violent Encounters*, a book by Anthony J. Pinizzotto, Edward F. Davis, and Charles Miller III, one paragraph, in particular, explains why police officers often have a hard time separating Hollywood fantasy from verifiable facts. In the real Old West, quick-draw gunfights were extremely rare.

Many of the officers interviewed for the present study lacked knowledge of human anatomy. They thought that, if forced into a situation where they must protect themselves or a member of the community, they could disable an offender quickly, effectively, and efficiently with their department-issued handguns. After lengthy discussions, the officers related that most of their real-world experience with gunshot wounds came from watching television and movies. (Published by the Federal Bureau of Investigation)

The following quote is from an article titled "One-shot Drops," which was written by Anthony J. Pinizzotto, Harry A. Kern, and Edward F. Davis and published in an FBI Law Enforcement Bulletin (October 2004, Volume 73, Number 10). The key to making a one-shot drop with a handgun is tactical anatomy, not caliber.

In the authors' ongoing study of violence against law enforcement officers, they have examined several cases where officers used large-caliber handguns with limited effect displayed by the offenders. In one case, the subject attacked the officer with a knife. The officer shot the individual four times in the chest; then, his weapon malfunctioned. The offender continued to walk toward the officer. After the officer cleared his weapon, he fired again and struck the subject in the chest. Only then did the offender drop the knife. This individual was hit five times with 230-grain, .45-caliber hollow-point ammunition and never fell to the ground. The offender later stated, "The wounds felt like bee stings."

If you compare training, elite military units have the most advanced tactical shooting skills, FBI and DEA agents have better than average tactical shooting skills, and most police officers have almost no tactical shooting skills. Elite military units usually have the most advanced tactical shooters because they have the best trainers, training facilities, and equipment, and they fire thousands of rounds per year.

If you compare annual qualification requirements, federal agents qualify four times per year, and most police officers qualify once per year. Shooting is a perishable skill. You cannot maintain or improve shooting skills without practice.

LISTEN TO THE EXPERTS

It's not surprising that many of the most significant advances in tactical shooting were made by military people because these experts used their combat experience to validate their methods and theories. Since some of the books authored by these veterans do not mention their military credentials, we would like to acknowledge their military service by listing their names and titles:

- Major General Julian S. Hatcher
- Captain William E. Fairbairn
- Captain E. A. Sykes
- Colonel Rex Applegate
- Colonel Jeff Cooper
- Colonel Charles Askins

In their book <u>Shooting to Live</u>, Captains Fairbairn and Sykes echo a view that was expressed by most of the combat veterans who are also champion target shooters: Much of what has been learned from target shooting "is best unlearned if proficiency is desired in the use of the pistol under actual fighting conditions."

We would also like to acknowledge Don Mann and Robert K. Taubert. Don Mann, a U.S. Navy SEAL and decorated combat veteran, wrote the book titled <u>The Modern Day Gunslinger</u>. According to Don Mann, point-shooting (target-focused shooting) is often used in gunfights and should be practiced in training. Many weapons instructors do not teach target-focused shooting, but research shows "there is little or no time for sighted techniques in most gunfights." Even people who normally use a front-sight focus often revert to point-shooting in a gunfight." In his book <u>Rattenkrieg!</u>, Robert K. Taubert—who was a U.S. Marine Corps veteran, Army Ranger, and retired FBI agent—agrees with Captains Fairbairn and Sykes: firearms competition is a game and "has little to do with reality."

If police departments didn't ignore the International Association of Chiefs of Police in 1971, the quality of police firearms training might be better than it is today. The following quote from an International Association of Chiefs of Police (IACP) training key #173 was published in 1971 and titled *Combat Shooting*.

- During a deadly confrontation, you must react automatically.
- In most combat situations, either you or your adversary will be moving.
- Breath control and a perfect stance are neither essential nor practical.
- You need to keep your eyes on the suspect, not on the front sight.

If police departments didn't ignore the IACP in 1971, today's police officers might not be getting killed because they don't know how to shoot a moving target or because they keep their eyes on the front sight instead of the suspect.

INTRODUCTION

People who believe they are tactical shooters because they have learned how to shoot paper targets and people who believe they have mastered hand-to-hand combat because they can do advanced katas often suffer from the same delusion: the belief that what they have learned will help them survive a deadly confrontation in the real world. This false and unfounded belief becomes painfully apparent when people from these two groups are faced with a deadly threat and find that none of the highly-valued skills they worked hard to learn work in the real world.

Police officers often realize how poor their training has been when they face someone with a gun or knife and use the skills they learned in the academy. Since the average hit rate for police officers is estimated to be about 30%, which means seven misses for every ten shots fired at a subject, you might believe police departments would improve their training methods—but you would be wrong.

Except for a few departments that have changed their approach to firearms training by making the training more realistic, giving their officers more time to practice, and raising qualification standards, many departments have decreased the quality of training because they are trying to save time or money.

Even when there is no correlation between high qualification scores and performance on the street, most police departments continue to ignore something that Albert Einstein said: "Insanity is doing the same thing over and over again and expecting different results." Poor training kills police and fails to protect the public.

This book explains the Porter Method, a reality-based and evidence-based approach to tactical handgun shooting. Many of the shooting and tactical skills in this book are based on combat-shooting techniques used as far back as the late 1700s. These techniques have been repeatedly field-tested and proven during actual combat. The people who have survived deadly encounters using these techniques are often the same people who write essays or books about them.

The Porter method was developed by examining gun techniques used by duelers, Old West gunfighters, combat veterans, and law enforcement officers. After examining these techniques, the next step was looking for ways to improve them.

Some of the techniques in this book might be controversial because many people still believe that target shooting and tactical shooting are the same, and we believe that tactical anatomy and shot placement are more important than using a large caliber handgun. The experts we respect are people like W. E. Fairbairn, E. A. Sykes, Rex Applegate, Jeff Cooper, Charles Askins, Jim Cirillo, and Paul Castle. A famous target shooter that we respect is Brian Enos. He does not claim to be a tactical shooter with combat experience, but he provides valuable information that will help tactical shooters have more control over their handguns.

It's common for the beliefs and recommendations made by one handgun expert to disagree with those made by other experts, and disagreements between experts can make it hard for the average person to know the difference between fact and fiction. When selecting techniques for this book, we considered facts, logic, science, research, and practical experience. We do not sell tactical products or club memberships. We do not recommend handguns or ammunition because the guns and ammunition we are using today might be considered outdated tomorrow.

As Bertrand Russell stated: "The fact that an opinion has been widely held is no evidence whatever that it is not utterly absurd; indeed, in view of the silliness of the majority of mankind, a widespread belief is more likely to be foolish than sensible." In other words, if conventional wisdom was always right, the earth would be flat, and the sun would rotate around the earth.

People who have never used a gun to win a deadly confrontation often view tactical shooting differently from those who used a gun for self-defense. Scientific research is a good source of information, but knowledge without practical experience is incomplete and often leads to the wrong conclusions. Techniques that have never been field-tested and proven are speculation, not fact.

When we created the Porter method, we did not use police firearms training as a model because most police departments' training is badly flawed and dangerous for the people who try to use it in the real world. *Fighting the way you train* does not work if what you were trained to do does not work. We disagree with many aspects of police firearms training and often use it to highlight techniques that might get you killed if you try to use them. Since both authors have been police officers and certified police instructors, we know that poor training can have fatal results.

We believe tactical shooting should be as natural and as simple as possible. Instead of teaching a target-shooting stance, such as the isosceles stance, we teach people to use the best stance possible under the circumstances. A good tactical stance provides stability and mobility. The isosceles stance might be the best for target shooters, but any stance that helps you make the first combat-effective hit will be the best for tactical shooters.

This book is more about flexible principles than rules because no two deadly confrontations are exactly the same. Sometimes you need to follow the US Marine Corps mantra: *improvise, adapt, and overcome.* Bad luck can work against you in a gunfight, but being able to adapt can help you improve your luck.

This book is for people who have completed basic handgun training and would like to become competent tactical shooters. Unlike experts who say a gunfight is nothing but a shooting match, we believe a gunfight is a thinking match. Tactical skills are more likely to save your life than shooting skills. If you put yourself in a position where you have no way to avoid being shot, you might never get a chance to use your shooting skills and make the first combat-effective shot.

POLICE FIREARMS TRAINING

It would be nice to use the firearms training police departments use as a model for tactical handgun training, but most of these programs are badly flawed and better for demonstrating what you should not do than what you should do. Except for the special units some departments have, which often receive training based on a military model instead of a police model, most of the firearms training police departments offer is not worth imitating.

Poor training partially explains why there is no correlation between being a top performer on a police target range and being combat-effective on the street. As Don Mann, a decorated combat veteran and Seal special operations technician, stated in a book he wrote titled <u>The Modern Day Gunslinger</u>, about 80% of the shots U.S. police officers fire are misses. If police officers had better firearms training, the hit rate for police officers would be higher.

Some of the training flaws that make it difficult for police officers to defend themselves during a deadly confrontation include:

- Using the isosceles stance instead of a tactical stance.
- Using silhouette targets that do not count headshots.
- Using center-of-mass instead of upper-chest targets.
- Using stationary paper targets that always face forward.
- Insufficient practice after graduating from the academy.
- Not teaching tactical skills when teaching shooting skills.
- Not teaching target-focused shooting.
- Not teaching how to shoot with both eyes open.
- Not teaching how to move and shoot at the same time.
- Not teaching one-handed shooting with the non-dominant hand.
- Not teaching how to shoot in a low-light or no-light environment.
- Not having a written use-of-force policy.
- Having a use-of-force policy that is more restrictive than state laws.
- Having a use-of-force policy that puts officers at a tactical disadvantage.
- Not covering legal fees when officers are sued because of using deadly force.

Based on tactical anatomy, police officers should earn more points for a head or upper chest shot than for center-of-mass shots. Because of their training, many police officers falsely believe that a center-of-mass will cause immediate incapacitation and stop a knife attack. The only two shots that usually cause immediate incapacitation are a shot that penetrates the brainstem or a shot that penetrates the upper cervical spinal cord. If a shot penetrates and stops the heart, a person attacking you might be fully functional for 10 to 15 seconds, which might be more than enough time for the person, to cut, stab, or shoot you.

One common mistake people make is believing a gunfight is nothing but a shooting match, and people who can punch holes in paper targets that do not shoot back have the skills they need to win a gunfight. On the contrary, a gunfight is a thinking match, and factors such as speed and accuracy are just parts of the process. In the real world, your brain should be running at full speed before you draw your gun, and you need to use your brain to get the tactical advantages you need to win the gunfight. In other words: no *brain, no gain.*

Another common mistake some people make is believing what they see on television or in the movies. The quick-draw showdowns you see in western movies seldom, if ever, occurred in the Old West, and actors are the only people who get knocked off their feet by one shot from a handgun. In the real world, handguns can run out of ammunition, and they are usually less accurate than a sniper rifle.

In the Old West, ambushing, shooting people in the back, or using a shotgun or rifle against a handgun was more common than standing face-to-face and testing your quick-draw skills. Some gunfights were won because the bad guys were too drunk to be fast or accurate, or their handguns or ammunition malfunctioned. Professional gunfighters tried to avoid fair fights because they realized a fair fight could get both shooters killed. Historically, the closest thing to a fair gunfight was a prearranged duel where both parties adhered to the rules.

Most of the breakthroughs that changed the nature of tactical shooting resulted from wartime combat experience. If you are fighting a war and soldiers are getting killed because of poor training, you change the way you train.

Tactical shooting made tremendous progress in the 1940s because of the work done by Colonel Rex Applegate when he was training World War II soldiers. When the military realized that traditional target-shooting techniques did not work under battlefield conditions, they brought in people, such as Colonel Applegate, who realized that target shooting and tactical shooting had very little in common.

After World War II, target shooting became more popular than tactical shooting, and police instructors were more likely to be target shooters than tactical shooters. A few tactical shooters realized that target shooting was more marketable than tactical shooting, and they became target shooting instructors.

One problem that occurs when you try to apply military training to a non-military situation is that you cannot use the same rules of engagement. What a military court calls *acceptable collateral damage*, a non-military court might call *the negligent killing of innocent bystander*s. Whereas the military, in most cases, tries to provide its soldiers with weapons equal to or more effective than the weapons used by the enemy, police departments have a long history of providing officers with weapons and ammunition that are less effective than what criminals are using. More than a few law enforcement officers have been killed because they were outgunned by criminals with high-capacity magazines or high-powered rifles.

New York City Police Department (NYPD)

The Firearms and Tactics Section of the NYPD released a report in 1981 called *SOP 9* that has a lot of valuable information about tactical shooting.

- Distance: Most police officers are shot and killed at less than 21 feet.
- Lighting: Dim lighting and highly-visible muzzle blast are common.
- Alignment of gun: A target focus was used in 70% or more of the cases.
- Quick draw: The gun was already drawn in about 65% of the cases.
- Cover: Using cover saved officers more than any other factor.
- Position: Most officers (84%) were in a standing or crouched position.
- One-hand shooting: Almost all the officers used their dominant hand.
- Warning shots: Firing a warning shot may encourage return fire.
- Running: Hits while running resulted from chance more than skill.
- Shots fired: Most officers did not fire more than three shots.
- Reload: Only 6% of the officers needed to reload.
- Ammunition: Shot placement was more important than the ammunition.
- Hit rate: About 25 hits for every 100 shots fired at assailants.
- Hitting a target at 150 feet does not help you hit the same target at 3 feet.
- There is no correlation between range score and tactical shooting skills.
- Training does not emphasize shooting targets at distances less than 21 feet.
- Point shooting (target-focused shooting) should be used at short distances.

Even though this report states that police officers use a target focus at least 70% of the time, most police departments do not show police officers how to use a target focus. Most police officers use a target focus when facing a deadly threat and a front-sight focus when shooting stationary paper targets.

Some departments believe having a fast draw is a major asset when someone threatens you with a knife, but most officers already have their guns drawn when facing a knife attack or any other deadly threat. When facing a knife attack, having your gun in your hand and good shot placement are more likely to save your life than reducing the time it takes for you to draw your gun by a fraction of a second.

Since using cover probably saves more lives than other factors, it's unclear why some police officers move away from cover when they shoot. If you are behind cover, try to stay behind cover when you shoot. If you are in the open when you shoot, try to *shoot and scoot*, which means quickly get behind cover after your shoot. Shooting with one hand instead of two can make it easier to keep more of your body behind cover when you shoot. If you use a vehicle for cover, try to stay behind the engine or wheels. The doors on some vehicles are better for concealment than cover.

SELF-DEFENSE

To say you have a legal right to use deadly force to protect yourself against a deadly threat might seem like an obvious truth until you try to define a *deadly threat*. If the United States Supreme Court tried to define a *deadly threat*, you would probably have several different opinions. And yet judges and juries expect law enforcement officers and civilians with no legal background to decide if they have a legal right to use deadly force in a fraction of a second.

This book can tell you how to improve your shooting or tactical skills, but we are not attorneys, and we cannot tell you when you have a legal right to use deadly force or if you will be charged with a crime or sued in civil court after using deadly force. Furthermore, predicting how a judge or jury will rule is almost impossible.

Different states may have different opinions concerning the elements of self-defense, such as when you have a duty to retreat, but here are some questions you might need to answer if you are trying to avoid prosecution by claiming that your use of deadly force was justified because of self-defense.

(**1**) Did you start, perpetuate, escalate, or agree to engage in the conflict?

(**2**) Did you have a reasonable belief the threat was imminent?

(**3**) Did you have a reasonable belief the threat would cause serious bodily harm.

(**4**) Was the force you used reasonable and necessary—but not excessive?

(**5**) Did you use force as a last resort because retreat was no longer possible or safe?

(**6**) Did you use deadly force to protect against an illegal threat of deadly force?

A force likely or intended to cause serious bodily injury or death is called *deadly force*, and the word *imminent* implies immediate or likely to happen at any moment. For a threat to be reasonable or credible, your attacker must have the ability (means and opportunity) to carry out the threat. In most cases, your attacker will also have a motive. *Excessive* implies the force used was unreasonable or unnecessary or that force was used after the threat stopped. If you claim a threat was deadly or imminent, you may need to show your beliefs were reasonable, prudent, or actual. Some states do not demand retreat when attacked in your home (Castle doctrine) or other special places, such as in your business or vehicle, but others might require retreat regardless of where you are. Even if it appears you had a legal right to use deadly force, it's almost impossible to predict a jury's verdict.

LEGENDARY GUNFIGHTERS

If you are trying to develop a realistic training program for tactical shooters, examining how gunfighters in the past survived gunfights is an excellent place to start. Handguns and ammunition have certainly improved over the past few hundred years, but the shooting skills and tactical skills gunfighters have used to stay alive are almost identical to the skills that will help a modern tactical shooter survive a gunfight. Because of the influence target shooters have had on tactical shooting, many of the tactical shooting skills police officers use are less effective than those used by legendary gunfighters, such as always using a front-sight focus.

Dueling and Old West Gunfighting

Duelists who fought with single-shot pistols never received the recognition in books or movies that gunfighters who used six-shot revolvers enjoyed, but the shooting skills that helped people survive a duel influenced the way Old West gunfighters and modern gunfighters use a handgun.

Single-shot, flintlock pistols used specifically for dueling appeared during the late 1700s. Misfires were very common, but a high-quality smoothbore dueling pistol could shoot a 2-inch group at 15 feet using a .50 to .60 caliber ball.

Dueling pistols did not always have sights, and they were held in one hand. To get a shot off quickly, you fired as soon as you raised the gun to eye level. Too much speed could result in missing a shot, and not enough speed could result in being dead before you fired a shot. The minimum time needed to fire an accurate shot tended to increase as the distance between the two adversaries increased. When fighting a duel at close range, speed was usually more important than carefully aligning the barrel of your pistol with your adversary.

Old West gunfighters also understood that the minimum time needed to fire a shot increased with distance. They often fanned the hammer and shot from the hip when they fought a close-quarter gunfight. On the other hand, when they were not involved in a close-quarter gunfight, they usually cocked the hammer, raised the barrel of their gun to eye level, and used their sights.

Having a hair trigger on a dueling pistol often caused accidental discharges because of nervous tension or inexperience. People familiar with dueling knew that hearing your adversary shoot might be sufficient to cause an involuntary contraction that activates the trigger before the gun was aimed. An experienced duelist would keep his finger off a hair trigger until the gun was aimed. To avoid accidental discharges, many police departments tell their officers to keep their fingers off the trigger until the gun is aimed at a potential target.

Using a target focus makes it easier to hit a moving target. Reasons for using a target focus were discussed in Helps and Hints: How to Protect Life and Property, which was written in 1835 by Lieutenant Colonel Baron De Berenger: "Self-defense requires rapid pistol shooting, and therefore precludes a deliberate aim along the barrel…." Baron De Berenger recommends that you look at your target when you shoot in the same way a swordsman watches his target when he strikes. Berenger also notes the similarity between target-focused shooting and pointing your finger.

Aiming is the process of pointing your gun at a target, and you can do this without focusing on the front sight to get a sight picture. Duelists with sights on their dueling pistols and Old West gunfighters like W.R (Bat) Masterson looked through their sights and then focused on their target. When shooting from the hip or shooting in a dark room where you cannot see your sights, your only option is to shoot without using your sights.

Most target shooters do not use or recommend target-focused shooting, but some of the best target shooters, such as Rob Leatham, use a target focus at close range. Police departments use a front-sight focus for close-range shooting because it reduces the risk that someone will fail to qualify.

If police departments what to improve the quality of their firearms training, officers should use front-sighed shooting at distances over 21 feet and target-focus shooting at distances 21 feet or closer. Most gunfights take place at less than 21 feet. A competent tactical shooter can use a target focus at distances greater than 21 feet, but a front-sight focus is more effective at distances greater than 75. Historians say the famous James Butler Hickok (Wild Bill Hickok) could raise his gun to eye level and use target-focused shooting at distances much greater than 75 feet.

This quote is from an essay written in 1875 titled <u>The Pistol as a Weapon of Defense in the House and on the Road</u>. The author is unknown, but Jeff Cooper wrote the foreword.

"Neither is it ever necessary to hit so small an object as a two-inch circle. He who can hit a four-inch circle at six paces will be master of the situation *provided he is quick enough*. But the aim, if aim it can be called, must be taken with the rapidity of thought; there must be no dallying to find the sights; no hesitation in the hope of bettering the aim. Delay, however occasioned, may cost us our life. Not that we would counsel hurry or want of coolness, for this will inevitably cause us to shoot wide of the mark. There is such a thing as being rapid, cool, and accurate, and this is what is needed."

The essay stated that dry-fire practice can reduce flinching, and having a good grip and using cover are important. The author also noted that unlike a bullet entering the heart, a bullet entering the head could be instantly fatal.

Most of what people believe about the legendary gunfighters in the Old West is fiction. Many of their deadly confrontations occurred because of whiskey, women, or gambling, and shooting people in the back was a popular tactic. Some gunfighters worked as both lawmen in one town and outlaws in other towns.

According to Joseph G. Rosa, who wrote The Gunfighters: Man or Myth? — most gunfighters had their pistol in their hand if they expected trouble, and quick-draw confrontations were extremely rare. If two gunfighters were equally skilled, they usually killed each other, which is why the gunfights between professionals were seldom fair fights.

Mr. Rosa also noted the better target shooter was not always the winner in a gunfight, and people with a killer instinct who didn't hesitate to shoot were more likely to win a gunfight than people with a less aggressive mindset. In a study that examined the characteristics of police officers who get killed in the line of duty, being less aggressive and using less force than other officers would use in a similar situation increases your risk of getting killed.

Several lessons can be drawn from Mr. Rosa's comments: (1) if possible, have your handgun out and ready before you get into a gunfight, (2) do not hesitate when you need to use deadly force, and (3) being aggressive can save your life.

Mr. Rosa also discusses the relationship between target shooting and tactical shooting. According to Walter Winans, a legendary target shooter in the late 1800s, shooting stationary targets, especially at long ranges, will not make you a better gunfighter. When using a handgun for self-defense, most of the shooting will be close range, your target will be moving, and the fight will be over in a few seconds.

Many people, including the famous Wyatt Earp, believed Wild Bill Hickok was the deadliest gunfighter who ever lived. If that's true, Wyatt Earp was not far behind. Both men were excellent marksmen and had nerves of steel, and neither man believed fanning a gun or using fast and fancy hip shooting was the way to win a gunfight. In a book titled Wyatt Earp, Stuart N. Lake, who did an authorized biography of Earp's life, makes some comments about Wyatt Earp and gunfights.

According to Mr. Lake, when Wyatt Earp said take your time, he meant you need to be mentally deliberate, but your muscles need to move faster than thought. Do not rush a shot and miss, but do not take more than a *split fraction of a second* to get your gun correctly aligned. Wyatt Earp did not believe in using techniques like fanning a gun or hip shooting. Like most gunfighters, he probably used a target focus during close-quarter gunfights and held his gun in front of his body with his forearm about level and his bent elbow held at or slightly above the waist. In a book titled The Gunfighters by Paul Trachtman, Bat Masterson said gunfighters practiced with guns the way card sharps practice with cards, and they practiced enough to make their movements smooth, lightning-fast, and automatic.

Many of the tactical shooting techniques used 150 years ago are still effective today, and most Old West gunfighters and target shooters realized that being a good target shooter does not make you a good gunfighter. Most police departments ignore the tactics that duelists and old west gunfighters used to stay alive and teach their officers basic target shooting instead of tactical pistol shooting.

Some people believe high-quality firearms training is too expensive and not worth the effort. On the other hand, lawsuits that result when a police officer kills an innocent civilian because of poor training can be very expensive. Many of the police officers killed in the line of duty would still be alive if their department were training tactical shooing instead of target shooting.

When state-required qualification standards are low, most police departments are not motivated to improve firearms training. The cost of ammunition can also be a problem. Serious target shooters fire hundreds of rounds per year, whereas the average police officer might not fire 50 rounds per year. Specialized units, such as Special Response Team, shoot more rounds per year than the average police officer and usually have much higher hit rates.

Many of the Old West lawmen who were good gunfighters, such as Wyatt Earp, could remain calm and focused during a gunfight. Staying calm and focused when under pressure did not always apply to their personal lives. Police officers who are usually calm and focused when performing regular duties sometimes become reckless or irrational when facing a deadly threat. Police officers who cannot control their emotions or actions when facing a deadly threat are unlikely to be competent tactical shooters regardless of what kind of training they get.

Police officers who are well-trained and have confidence in their shooting skills and handguns are less likely to panic during a deadly confrontation than poorly trained officers who have little confidence in their shooting skills or handguns. Officers who have not been trained to shoot a moving target may panic and start shooting if it looks like someone with a knife may start running toward them. Police officers who always use a front-sight focus may fail to shoot someone who attacks them with a knife because they can't see someone is holding a knife because their eyes are focused on their front sight.

When Old West gunfighters shooting at a distance brought their gun up to eye level, they were careful not to cover their target with any part of their gun. If you use a front-sight focus when making a headshot, it will be hard to see which way the head is moving if most of the front sight covers your head.

You should not carry a handgun for self-defense until you have test-fired the gun and know the relationship between your sighs and a target. Your front sight should be slightly below your target instead of covering your target. If you use fixed sights and the front sight covers most of your target, you need to change your sights or have a professional gunsmith adjust your sights.

Modern Gunfighters: Use a Target Focus

In No Second Place Winner, Bill Jordan made another statement that leads you to question why anyone with practical experience who had used a handgun for self-defense would recommend using front-sight focus at close range.

According to Mr. Jordan, who wrote No Second Place Winners, many of the affrays between police officers and criminals take place at close range and involve the element of surprise or poor lighting, which makes deliberate aimed fire not only inadvisable but impossible.

Jim Cirillo, who was on a famous New York Stakeout Squad, realized that using a target focus is better than using a front-sight focus in most tactical situations and that tactical shooting rewards combat-effective accuracy instead of precision accuracy. Cirillo stated that if you are shooting at a great distance, you need to use your front sight, but if you are shooting toe-to-toe, you need to be looking at your target and *not waste time seeking out the sights*. If you are focused on your front sight, you cannot see if a poor guy in front of you is pulling out his wallet or a gun. Many of Cirillo's students could achieve combat effectiveness at close range when the sights on their guns were covered with tape.

In their book Deadly Force, William Geller and Michael Scott stated there is no correlation between the police hitting the people they shoot at and qualifying scores. In his book Combat Shooting, Massad Ayoob made a similar observation. In The Officer Survival Manual, Devallis Rutledge stated target shooting promotes familiarity with your weapon but will not help you win a gunfight. In Fast and Fancy Revolver Shooting and Police Training, Ed McGivern stated that competent handgun training could save lives and prevent unnecessary killings. People with good tactical shooting skills are less likely to panic and make deadly mistakes.

W. E Fairbairn, E. A. Sykes, and Rex Applegate are military handgun experts. These men believed that target-focused shooting is more practical than front-sight-focused shooting in most tactical situations. Many of the techniques they used are in a book by Colonel Rex Applegate and Michael D. Janich titled Bullseyes Don't Shoot Back. Some of the techniques they recommend are shooting with both eyes open and using a combat crouch. In Kill or Get Killed, Colonel Applegate stated target shooting would not prepare you for combat, and police departments spend too much time on target shooting and not enough time teaching skills that will save a police officer's life.

In the Textbook of Pistols and Revolvers, Major General Julian Hatcher said a front-sight focus could be useful if time permits and the target is not close or very small. If a target is close and not small, using a target focus will be more effective. In his book The Art of Handgun Shooting, Colonel Askins stated that using a target focus is usually better than a front-sight focus if your life is in jeopardy.

All the modern gunfighters mentioned agreed that most police departments teach target shooting instead of tactical shooting. Many police departments believe that high-quality firearms training is too expensive and would take too much time. Some departments believe other types of training are more critical than firearms training and that any firearms training program that helps police officers meet minimum state standards is good enough.

Better police firearms training would reduce the number of police officers killed in the line of duty and reduce the number of innocent civilians killed because of accidental or unnecessary shootings. Most firearms experts would strongly agree.

This list summarizes what competent duelists and gunfighters believe:

- Most deadly confrontations occur at close range.
- Use a target focus when a target is close and moving.
- Use a target focus when you have limited light or no light.
- Use a front-sight focus when a target is distant or small.
- Most target shooters use a front-sight focus.
- Most tactical shooters use a target focus more than a front-sight focus.
- A tactical shooter should learn how to shoot with both eyes open.
- Being a good target shooter will not make you a tactical shooter.
- A tactical shooter needs realistic practice.
- Correct and frequent practice will improve your shooting skills.

Despite what the experts say, most police departments continue to pretend that target shooting is the same as tactical shooting and that meeting state qualification standards makes you a tactical shooter. Most trainees can meet state qualification standards after one week of firearms training. Even if they have good shooting skills, most police officers will not be able to stop a knife attack because they don't understand tactical anatomy or shot placement. Despite what many police officers believe, bullets that penetrate the body's center of mass are unlikely to stop a knife or gun attack. Even if a shot stops the heart, someone who attacks you with a knife or gun might be functional for 10 or 15 seconds and have time to complete the attack.

You can teach tactical shooting without having an expensive training facility. When shooting at 75 feet, you can use a steel silhouette target with a 5-inch gong. When shooting at less than 75 feet, it's usually safer to have a 5-inch paper plate on a paper silhouette than to use steel targets. A shot needs to hit inside the 5-inch target for the shot to count. Most shooting should be done with a target focus. If you can hit a 5-inch target at 45 feet when using a target focus, you stand a good chance of making a headshot that will stop a knife attack.

SHOT PLACEMENT

If you are faced with a deadly threat, causing *incapacitation* means doing something that stops someone from threatening you with deadly force. A threat is considered deadly when it's capable of causing serious bodily harm or death. When faced with a deadly threat, police officers normally use a handgun, shotgun, or rifle to counteract the threat. Most police officers use a handgun to counteract a deadly threat, but a tactical rifle or a 12-gauge shotgun with buckshot or a shotgun slug will usually cause more tissue damage than a standard police handgun.

Incapacitation can be immediate or timely. *Immediate incapacitation* stops a deadly threat instantly, and *timely incapacitation* stops a deadly threat before it causes serious bodily harm or death. A shot that disrupts the brainstem or upper cervical spinal cord causes immediate incapacitation and usually death. A shot that disrupts the lower cervical spinal cord might cause immediate incapacitation because of paralysis. A shot that stops the heart might cause timely incapacitation if the attacker cannot complete the attack in less than 10 or 15 seconds.

Incapacitation can also be *permanent* or *temporary*. If a spinal cord injury causes immediate incapacitation, the incapacitation can be permanent or temporary. A bullet penetrating the intestines might not cause immediate incapacitation, but the wound might cause permanent incapacitation or death days after the gunshot wound because of inflammation from peritonitis.

Temporary incapacitation might be caused by a bullet that glances off the skull and causes temporary unconsciousness because of the blunt trauma. If you react appropriately, you might be able to take advantage of the situation and stop the person from being a deadly threat. Your next best option might be using cover or concealment to strengthen your position.

Do not relax too soon and do nothing to protect yourself if your assailant is temporarily incapacitated. Even if help is on the way, it might not arrive soon enough to be much help. Try to remove any weapons that can be used against you if you can do it without risking injury. If you cannot safely approach your assailant, try to find cover, reload if necessary, and be prepared to shoot.

Do not assume someone who falls and appears to be unconscious after you shoot is not a threat. Some people will fall even when they are not hit, and others will pretend to be unconscious and hope you get careless.

Having the right to use deadly force to protect yourself from a deadly threat does not give you the right to commit murder. When deadly force is necessary, the objective is to cause immediate or timely incapacitation, not immediate or eventual death. After an injured person is no longer a threat, discontinue using force, render first aid if possible, and call for medical assistance if needed.

Headshot

To achieve combat effectiveness, the actions you take when facing a deadly threat need to neutralize the threat by causing immediate or timely incapacitation. A 5-inch group can be just as combat-effective as a 2-inch group if you select the right aim point and your bullet penetrates far enough to reach the critical tissues.

If your aim point is the traditional *center of mass*, none of the shots that hit the aim point will cause immediate incapacitation, and most of them will not cause timely incapacitation because your chances of hitting critical tissues are very small. Center of mass is a good aim point if you are trying to qualify at the range, but it's not a good aim point if you are trying to cause immediate or timely incapacitation.

The only two shots that reliably cause immediate incapacitation are those that penetrate the brainstem (midbrain, pons, and medulla oblongata) or the upper cervical spinal cord. The upper cervical spine is the aim point, but the upper cervical spinal cord is the target. The neck has seven cervical vertebrae, and the upper four—C1, C2, C3, and C4—protect the upper cervical spine. C1 connects with an opening in the skull (occipital bone) called the foramen magnum.

The first cervical vertebra is just below the base of the skull when viewed from the back, and the last cervical vertebra (C7) is the bump you feel when you run your hand down the back of your neck. The third cervical vertebra is about level with the bottom of your chin when your head is level. The aim points for a headshot are the middle of the bridge of the nose, the ear canals (external auditory meatus), and the occipital protuberance (bump) above the foramen magnum.

When the ear canal is used as an aim point, any shot that misses and passes through facial bones, such as the jaw bone (mandible), will not cause significant incapacitation. If a person is standing erect, a shot that goes slightly over the top of the ear will usually cause immediate or timely incapacitation. The aim point for a headshot is a 5-inch circle, but you have a margin of error because a bullet slightly high or low may still cause timely or immediate incapacitation.

To practice headshots, think of a 5-inch band going around the head with an imaginary line dividing the top half from the bottom half. To position this band on the head, place the imaginary line over the middle of the nasal bridge, over both ear canals, and over the occipital bump (protuberance), which is just above the juncture between the back of the skull and the neck. Regardless of where you are standing, the aim point is a line that divides a 5-inch band into two 2.5-inch bands. If you are standing in front of the head, the aim point would be the nose bridge, if you are standing to the side, the aim point would be an ear canal, and if you are standing behind the head, the aim point would be the occipital bump. If you are standing at any other angle, the aim point would be somewhere between two standard aim points. When aiming at the band, aim halfway between the top and bottom.

Bullets that penetrate the brainstem cause immediate incapacitation because of flaccid paralysis that stops muscle contractions, and bullets that go just over the brainstem and hit the basal ganglia may cause immediate incapacitation because of a loss of consciousness and the inability to move. Even if they eventually cause incapacitation, bullets that hit higher parts of the brain might cause involuntary muscle contractions because of reflex activity that is strong enough to pull a trigger and kill a hostage. Besides causing quadriplegia (tetraplegia), a bullet that penetrates the upper spinal cord can cause death if damage to the phrenic nerve or paralysis of the intercostal muscles or diaphragm terminates normal breathing.

Bullets that sever the spinal cord below C4 may cause a loss of motor function below the level of the injury, and bullets that penetrate the carotid artery or jugular vein may cause death because of hemorrhage. Bullets that hit the windpipe (trachea) or cause profuse bleeding may obstruct breathing, but bullets that penetrate neck muscles might not cause any significant loss of function.

Because the cranium confines the brain, a sudden rise in intracranial pressure may cause immediate death, but high-velocity rifle bullets are more likely to have this effect than handgun bullets unless the end of a handgun barrel is making solid contact with the head when the gun is fired. Contact and near-contact wounds are usually the results of suicide or execution.

The damage from a handgun bullet might be greater than expected if the bullet penetrates but fails to exit the skull and ricochets off the skull's inner surface (table) or glides along the inner surface. Bullets that hit but fail to penetrate the skull may cause fractures or concussions. The severity of these injuries can range from minor damage to immediate incapacitation or death if the concussion affects the brainstem.

If the impact angle is within 10 degrees of being parallel to the skull, the bullet may cause only minor flesh damage and glance off. Unlike the large-caliber lead balls used in flintlock pistols, modern ammunition will usually penetrate any part of the skull, including the frontal bone, if the impact angle is within 10 degrees of being perpendicular to the skull.

Headshots or shots that sever the upper cervical spine are the only reliable way to cause immediate incapacitation. A neck shot that severs the upper cervical spine will cause immediate incapacitation, but neck shots are harder to make than headshots. The primary targets when using a handgun are the head and upper chest.

When training to make a headshot, a realistic size for a bullseye is 5 inches. When practicing with a 5-inch bullseye, a shot that touches the edge of the bullseye is counted as a miss. It's easier to make a frontal or lateral headshot than a frontal or lateral heart shot because the head is easy to see, and the chest conceals the heart and the major arteries surrounding the heart. About 40% of the people killed by criminals are shot in the head, and about 25% are shot in the heart. Police snipers use headshots because they cause immediate incapacitation.

Headshots accounted for about 49% of the law enforcement officers fatally wounded by criminals from 2001 to 2010. Headshots killed about 57% of the police officers who wore body armor during the same period. The Federal Bureau of Investigation (FBI) chart below shows that criminals often use headshots.

Except for the members of a tactical unit, most police officers have never been trained to use headshots. Headshots are the best way to stop a violent criminal wearing a bullet-resistant vest, but most police officers do not have the shooting skills or the knowledge of shot placement they need to make a headshot that causes immediate incapacitation. Shooting a hip or thigh shot will not stop an active shooter from killing you, although an active shooter might die within several minutes if a bullet severs the femoral artery.

**Law Enforcement Officers Feloniously Killed with Firearms
Location of Fatal Firearm Wound and
Number of Victim Officers Wearing Body Armor 2001-2010**

	Location of fatal firearm wound	Total	2001	2002	2003	2004	2005	2006	2007	2008	2009	2010
Number of victim officers killed with firearms	Total	498	61	51	45	54	50	46	56	35	45	55
	Front head	141	27	14	9	10	17	10	18	9	16	11
	Rear head	42	3	8	5	6	6	5	3	1	2	3
	Side head	62	4	7	7	7	2	5	7	8	5	10
	Neck/throat	45	3	3	5	3	5	7	2	5	7	5
	Front upper torso/chest	136	16	12	12	19	14	11	19	7	11	15
	Rear upper torso/back	21	3	1	3	0	2	3	5	1	1	2
	Front lower torso/stomach	31	5	3	3	4	3	2	1	4	1	5
	Rear lower torso/back	9	0	1	0	3	1	1	1	0	0	2
	Front below waist	5	0	1	1	0	0	2	0	0	1	0
	Rear below waist	4	0	1	0	2	0	0	0	0	0	1
	Arms/hands	0	0	0	0	0	0	0	0	0	0	0
	Fatal wound location not reported	2	0	0	0	0	0	0	0	0	1	1

Number of victim officers killed with firearms while wearing body armor	Total (2001- 2010)	324	38	34	31	31	30	26	34	29	33	38
	Front head	108	21	12	6	5	12	9	15	9	12	7
	Rear head	29	1	5	3	5	4	3	2	1	2	3
	Side head	47	2	4	5	3	2	3	7	6	5	10
	Neck/throat	36	3	3	4	3	3	4	1	4	6	5
	Front upper torso/chest	72	9	4	8	11	8	6	7	5	7	7
	Rear upper torso/back	7	1	0	1	0	0	1	1	1	1	1
	Front lower torso/stomach	15	1	3	3	1	1	0	0	3	0	3
	Rear lower torso/back	5	0	1	0	2	0	0	1	0	0	1
	Front below waist	2	0	1	1	0	0	0	0	0	0	0
	Rear below waist	3	0	1	0	1	0	0	0	0	0	1
	Arms/hands	0	0	0	0	0	0	0	0	0	0	0

Police officers often have a problem knowing where to aim when someone who appears to be a deadly threat is not facing them. This problem is usually the result of shooting paper targets that are always facing them. A police officer who wants to progress beyond target shooting needs to know the aim points when you are behind or beside someone and then practice hitting these aim points. Unlike police officers who usually expose the front of their body when they shoot, criminals who shoot while running away will expose the back or the side of their body.

Regardless of which side of a body you are facing, the aim point for a headshot will usually be close to the center of the head and level with one or both ears. If the only part of a body you can see is the side, the aim point for an upper chest shot will be the armpit. If the only part of a body you can see is the back, the aim point will be where a line drawn from one armpit to the other crosses the spine. If you face someone and your bodies are almost pressed together, you can use the area under the chin for an aim point and shoot upward toward the brainstem.

If you have one hand on your adversary's knife or gun and your gun is in the other hand, it's safer to raise your gun and try to hit the brainstem or upper cervical spinal cord by shooting upward into the space under the chin than aim for the nose bridge or ear canal.

When shooting upward, you can keep your elbow pointed down and use your forearm to protect your body while the other arm tries to control your adversary's weapon. If you cannot hit the space under the chin, try to hit the heart. If you are using a semiautomatic pistol, keep in mind that pressing the barrel against your adversary may push the slide back (out of battery) and prevent the gun from firing.

Headshots that are too high to hit the brainstem or basal ganglia might damage critical tissues enough to cause timely incapacitation. The impact from a bullet hitting the skull's outer surface may cause impact damage. A bullet that hits the frontal bone at close to a perpendicular angle will usually penetrate the skull if the ammunition can penetrate 10% ballistic gelatin at least 12 inches.

Bullets that hit the frontal bone have been known to glance off or stop before they penetrate the skull, but using ammunition with good penetration will increase your chances of penetrating the skull and causing timely incapacitation. Bullets that tumble or ricochet after penetrating the skull may cause massive tissue damage.

A handgun bullet hits the body with about the same force as a fast-moving baseball, and just the impact from a bullet hitting the temple might be fatal. Blunt trauma to the temporal area of the skull may cause unconsciousness or death if it fractures the temporal bone, ruptures a meningeal artery, and causes intracranial hemorrhage. The temporal region is not used as an aim point because a bullet that hits this area is less likely to cause immediate incapacitation than a bullet that hits the brainstem. Bullets that penetrate the temporal bone do not always cause death. One woman lived for three months after she shot herself in the temple.

Heart Shot: Heart and Thoracic Spine

The heart shot aim point is a 4-inch circle near the center of the sternum and between a man's nipples. Two-thirds of the heart is on the left side of the body, but shooting to the left reduces your chances of hitting the spinal cord. If you add the large blood vessels above the heart, such as the aorta (aortic arch), to the heart's height, you can make the aim point a 5-inch-circle. Bullets that hit the aorta may cause more internal bleeding than bullets that hit the heart.

Psychological factors or drug usage can affect how quickly a bullet that penetrates (enters) or perforates (enters and exits) your adversary's heart causes incapacitation. Even if a bullet completely stops the heart, the body can remain functional for 10 to 15 seconds, which is more than enough time to return fire and cause a fatal gunshot wound. If the heart, aorta, or pulmonary arteries or veins are severely damaged, unconsciousness may occur in less than 30 seconds.

Bullets that hit the heart do not always cause permanent incapacitation or death. Some people can stay conscious and functional for much longer than 15 seconds after a bullet penetrates their heart, and with immediate medical treatment, they might survive and fully recover. According to Doctors Wiener and Barrett, who wrote <u>Trauma Management</u>, high-velocity bullets (2000 to 2500 feet per second) that penetrate the heart may cause immediate incapacitation and death—but most handgun bullets will not have a similar effect. High-velocity rifle bullets are faster and produce more kinetic energy than most handgun bullets. High-velocity rifle bullets tend to travel sideways (yaw), tumble, or fragment more than handgun bullets, making them more lethal than most handgun bullets.

When making a heart shot, the primary target is the heart, and the secondary target is the thoracic spine. If a target faces you, the bullet will hit the heart before hitting the spine. If you are behind a target, the bullet will hit the spine before hitting the heart. A bullet with shallow penetration might stop after penetrating the sternum and heart or stop after penetrating the vertebrae and spine.

The upper chest (thorax), which is between the neck and abdomen, is the aim point for the heart and surrounding tissue. The space between the scapulas is the posterior (back) aim point for the heart and surrounding tissues. The lower border of the axilla (armpit) is the aim point for the heart and surrounding tissue when a target is standing sideways. If your shot is high and you hit the neck, the shot might cause incapacitation or death because of penetrating a large blood vessel or the upper cervical spinal cord. If you shoot low and penetrate the abdomen or shoot to the side a penetrate a lung, the wounds might not be immediately noticed or fatal.

The heart is below the center of the sternum, and more of the heart is to the left of the sternum than to the right, but firing two shots at the heart instead of one will increase your combat effectiveness more than aiming at the left side of the heart.

Pelvic Shot: Pelvis and Lumbar Spine

If you have a choice, a head or heart shot will be more combat effective than a pelvic shot. If someone is wearing a high-quality, tactical bullet-resistant helmet, face mask, and vest, or if the only part of the body that's exposed is the lower body, your best option might be a pelvic shoot. Pelvis shots made with a shotgun or high-velocity are usually far more devastating than a pelvic shot made with a handgun.

The hip joint is a ball and socket joint that connects a leg to the body. The hip joints are on the sides of the pelvis. The pelvis is on one side of the hip joint, and the upper leg bone (femur) is on the other side.

Causing immobility by fracturing the pelvis or the head of a femur with a handgun bullet is possible but unlikely. The hip joint is hard to hit because it's small (about two inches in diameter) and hard to see even when it's not covered by clothing. Handgun bullets that strike the hip joint seldom cause significant instability unless they break the neck of the femur.

The aim point for a pelvic shot is not a hip joint if you are using a handgun. When viewed from the front or back, the aim point for a pelvic shot is the juncture between the fourth and fifth lumbar vertebrae. These lumbar bones are at about the same level as the top of your hip bone (iliac crest). Most people wear a belt slightly above the top of their hip bones, although a tactical belt might rest on your hips. If you use a belt to determine the aim point for a pelvic shot, the center of the 5-inch aim point should be close to the bottom of a belt and the lumbar vertebrae cross.

A bullet will not damage the 18-inch spinal cord because it ends at the lower border of the first lumbar vertebrae, but you may damage a collection of spinal nerve roots called the *cauda equina* that descends from the bottom of the spinal cord. Damage to these nerves may affect leg or foot movements and cause paraplegia. A pelvic shot that severs the abdominal aorta may cause unconscious in less than 60 seconds—which might be enough time to fire several shots. It is safer to use a pelvic shot when your adversary's weapon is a knife instead of a gun.

In Jim Cirillo's Tales of the Stakeout Squad, a New York Stakeout Squad member used a handgun to shoot an armed robber five times in the vicinity of the belt buckle, and the suspect did not go down. Rather than fire more shots, the officer charged the suspect and knocked him down, which gave his partner a chance to get the suspect's gun. The book does not explain why these five shots did not cause incapacitation, but the suspect died a couple of hours later.

A pelvic shot might cause psychological incapacitation because of fear, pain, or the awareness of being shot, which may cause someone to surrender. Be careful how you approach someone who appears to be unconscious. If someone armed with a gun drops to the floor after a pelvic shot, getting behind cover might be your best option. Blood loss may indicate if the person is pretending to be unconscious.

Unexpected Incapacitation

Shock, which is caused by an inadequate blood supply to the brain, is one condition that might cause almost immediate incapacitation because of a minor wound or no wound. When caused by a bullet, shock is usually the result of bleeding and low blood volume (hypovolemic shock).

Psychogenic shock and *neurogenic shock* are caused by vascular dilation and a reduction of blood to the brain. Psychogenic shock is caused by psychological factors, such as severe pain or the sight of blood, and neurogenic shock can be caused by cerebral or spinal-cord trauma. Strong emotions, such as anger, rage, hate, or determination, might reduce the perception of pain and prevent psychogenic shock. People who didn't know they were shot might not show symptoms of psychogenic shock until someone tells them they are bleeding.

Neurologic shock can result from cerebral trauma or a spinal cord injury and cause a loss of blood pressure (hypotension). Spinal-cord injuries can also cause *spinal shock*, which disrupts the nerve supply below the level of the injury and causes an immediate but temporary loss of sensory and motor activity that might not last for more than one hour. A temporary loss of reflex activity and paralysis might cause enough incapacitation to stop a knife or gun attack.

A gunshot that damages an organ, such as the liver or spleen, or ruptures a large blood vessel, such as the abdominal aorta, may cause *hemorrhagic shock* if blood loss (hemorrhage) causes a rapid reduction in blood flow to the brain. Shock results if one-fifth to one-third of someone's blood volume is lost rapidly, and death usually occurs if half of someone's blood volume is lost rapidly (exsanguination). Multiple center-of-mass handgun shots might not cause hemorrhagic if none of the shots severely damage organs and large blood vessels.

Reasonable Force

Even after an autopsy, medical examiners are not always sure which shot was the cause of death and whether the shot that was the cause of death was the first or last shot fired. It's reasonable to continue shooting until you believe a person posing a deadly threat has incapacitated, but it's hard to know where the line is between not enough force and too much force. A well-placed headshot will cause immediate incapacitation, and a well-placed heart shot will cause timely or eventual incapacitation. A pelvic shot might cause a loss of mobility, and in some cases, might cause incapacitation because of blood loss. Predicting what multiple center-of-mass hits will cause is almost impossible because it's hard to predict which organs or large blood vessels were hit. Increasing the number of center-of-mass hits you make will increase your chances of causing timely incapacitation.

Anterior and Posterior Aim Points

The three aim points are where the lines cross.

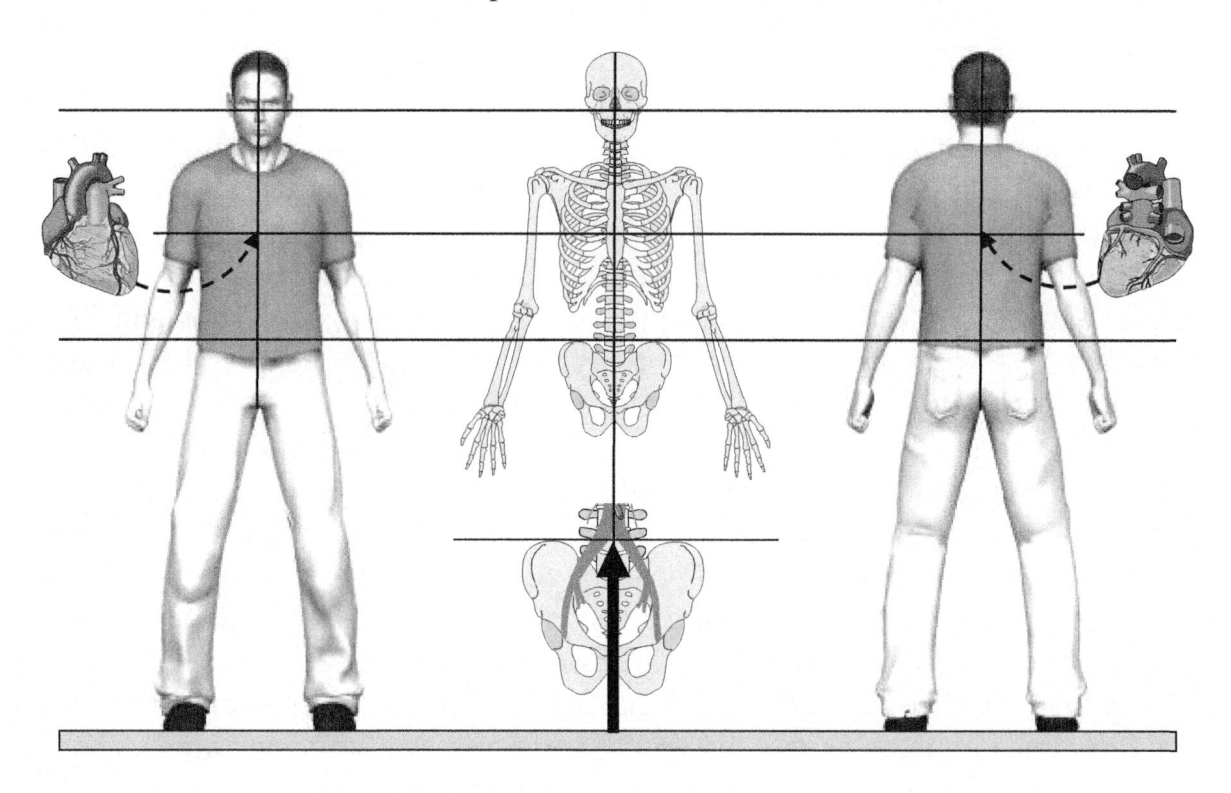

Aim point one—Nose Bridge. This 5-inch aim point covers the brainstem and the upper cervical spine. A bullet that goes slightly over the top of the brainstem may hit the basal ganglia, and one that goes below the head may hit the neck. Disrupting the brainstem, basal ganglia, or the upper cervical spinal cord above C4 causes immediate incapacitation.

Aim point two: This 5-inch aim point covers the heart and the major blood vessels near the heart, such as the aorta or vena cava, and the thoracic spine. A bullet that hits the aorta may cause incapacitation faster than a bullet that penetrates the heart. A person will usually be fully functional for about 10 to 15 seconds if a bullet stops the heart. Severing the thoracic spinal cord may cause a loss of mobility.

Aim point three: This 5-inch aim point covers the first sacral vertebrae, lumbar vertebrae, and blood vessels such as the abdominal aorta or iliac artery. As indicated by the arrow, the center of this aim point is on the same level as the top of the pelvis (iliac crest). Hitting this aim point may cause a loss of mobility and possibly death if the bullet hits a large blood vessel. Clothing can make it hard to find this aim point, and hits might not cause immediate immobility.

Lateral Aim Points and Center of Mass

These 5-inch aim points are where the lines cross. The head aim point is the ear, which should be easy to see from the side. The heart aim point is the armpit, which might be hard to see from the side if it's covered by an arm. The pelvic aim is the top of the pelvis, which might be very hard to see from the side if it's covered by clothing. A hip or knee joint shot might be more practical than a pelvic shot.

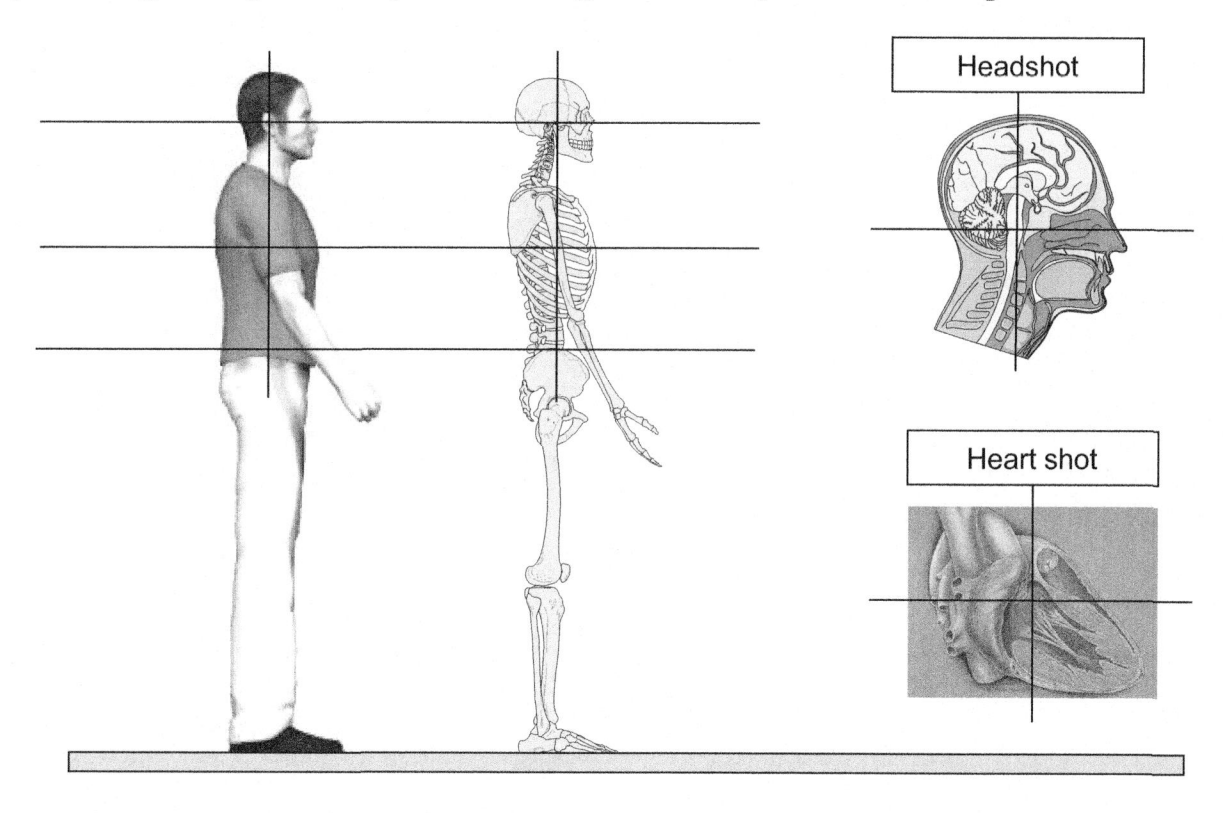

The areas enclosed by ovals are often included as part of the *center of mass*. Multiple hits to these areas are unlikely to cause immediate incapacitation. If the torso is considered part of the center of mass, bullets that penetrate a lung might not have any immediate effects.

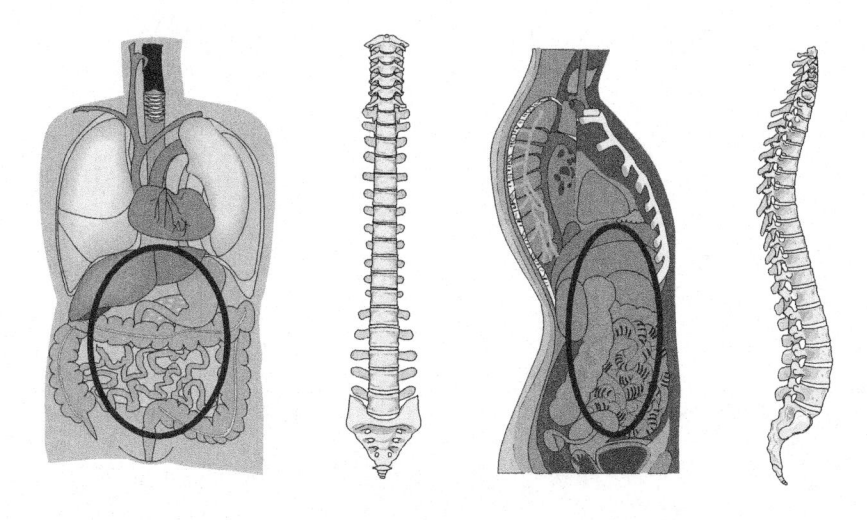

Brainstem and Upper Spine Aim Points

The only way to cause immediate incapacitation with a handgun is to fire a bullet that penetrates the brainstem or upper cervical spine. Even though most police departments do not teach or recommend headshots, from most angles, it's easier to make a headshot than a heart shot. Unlike a heart shot, a headshot causes immediate incapacitation instead of timely or eventual incapacitation. The illustration below shows easy it is to make a headshot from several different angles.

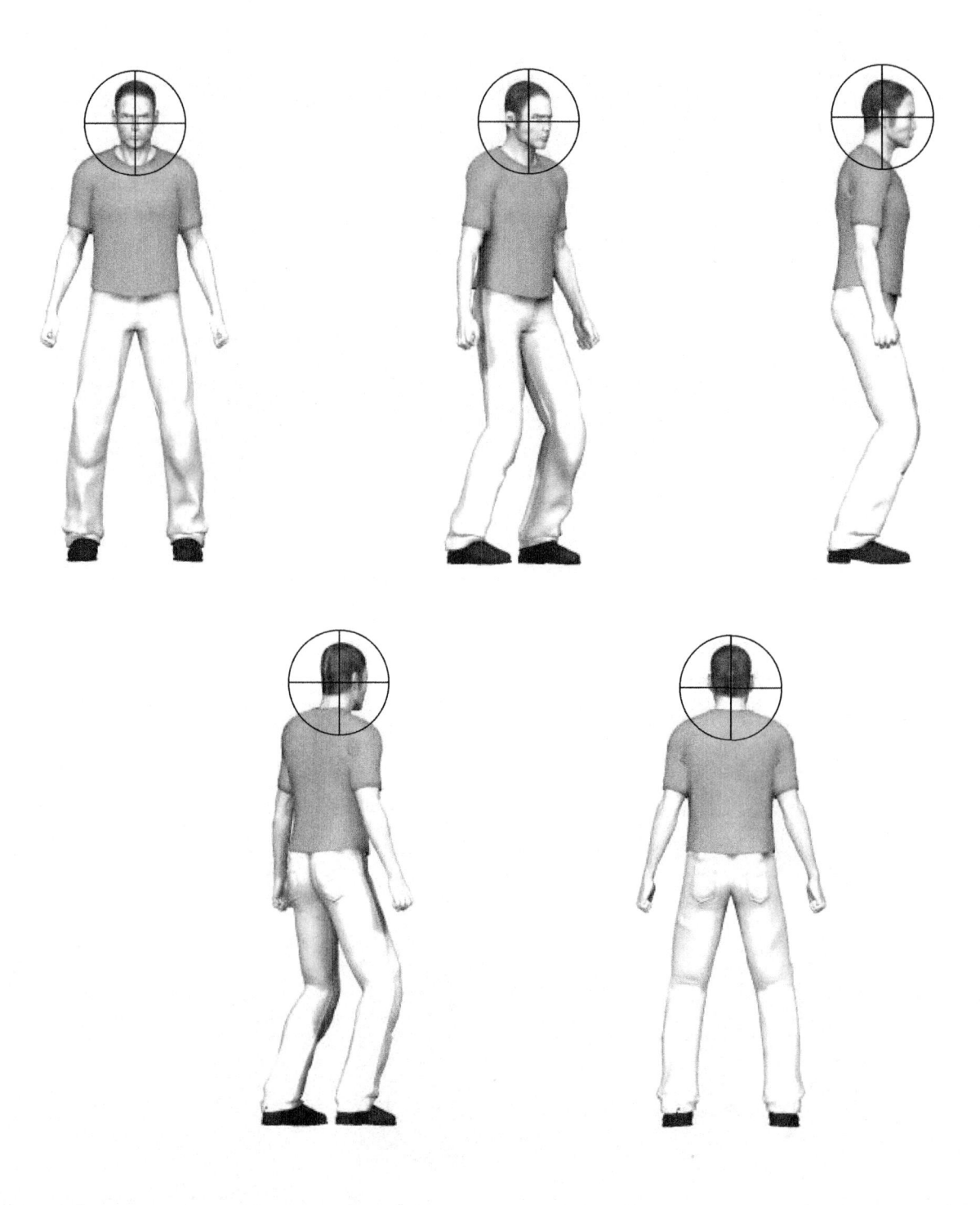

28

Avoid Target Shooter Aim Points

If your goal is to be a tactical shooter, you should use targets based on tactical anatomy. If you use targets that give you full credit for hitting the center of mass, you are training yourself to shoot at body parts that are unlikely to cause immediate or timely incapacitation if you manage to hit them. If you do not get any credit for making a headshot, you are training yourself not to shoot at the one body part that usually causes immediate incapacitation.

In *The Modern Technique of the Pistol*, written by Gregory Morrison and edited by Jeff Cooper in 1991, Dr. Morrison states:

"Initially, someone may take offense to the brain shot being described so matter-of-factly. One should not be indifferent to the loss of life that is likely to result from such a wound….Some people must be dealt with in harsh ways in order to save innocent lives….Do not forfeit your life, or someone else's, just because you find some aspects of defensive pistolcraft distasteful."

Since we are not attorneys or politicians, we cannot comment on whether using a headshot to save yourself or someone else is legal or politically correct. Based on forensic science and tactical anatomy, we can tell you that a headshot almost always causes immediate incapacitation, and a center-of-mass shot almost never causes immediate incapacitation.

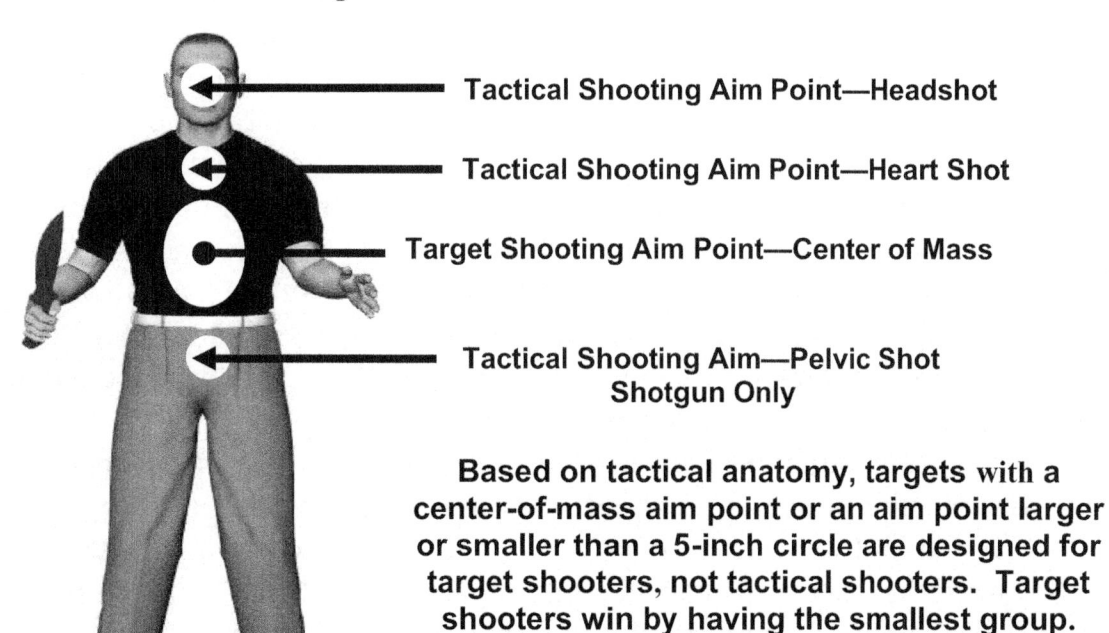

Tactical Shooting Aim Point—Headshot

Tactical Shooting Aim Point—Heart Shot

Target Shooting Aim Point—Center of Mass

Tactical Shooting Aim—Pelvic Shot
Shotgun Only

Based on tactical anatomy, targets with a center-of-mass aim point or an aim point larger or smaller than a 5-inch circle are designed for target shooters, not tactical shooters. Target shooters win by having the smallest group. Tactical shooters win by making the first combat-effective shot.

Summary

If you are facing an imminent deadly threat and you want to use a handgun to cause immediate incapacitation, the four essential elements are represented by the acronym *ASAP*:

- *A*—aim point: only a headshot will cause immediate incapacitation.
- *S*—speed: you need to shoot before your adversary shoots (quick or dead).
- *A*—accuracy: you need to make a combat-effective headshot.
- *P*—penetration: the bullet needs to reach the brainstem or upper cervical spine.

The winner of a gunfight is the first to fire a combat-effective headshot. If you are too slow and your adversary makes a combat-effective headshot before you do, you lose. If you miss and fire a shot that is not combat effective and your adversary fires a combat effective headshot, you lose.

Target shooters usually have a certain amount of time to place their shots as close to the center of a bullseye as possible. Tactical shooters are more concerned about being faster than their adversaries than operating within a time limit. A target shooter usually needs to shoot a tight group near the center of a bullseye to win. The tactical shooter who makes the first combat-effective headshot, which means putting a shot anywhere within a 5-inch circle, wins. A target shooter can use ammunition that is just powerful enough to penetrate a piece of paper. A tactical shooter needs to use ammunition that has enough power to penetrate the skull and reach the brainstem and upper cervical spine. It should be evident that training to be a target shooter will not be the same as training to be a tactical shooter.

Most police departments teach their officers to shoot at the center of mass even though numerous cases have occurred where multiple shots to the torso with large-caliber handgun bullets did not stop a criminal from killing a police officer. It's hard to say how many officers have been killed because no one used a headshot when a criminal was close enough to make a headshot easy, such as when a criminal is trying to take your partner's handgun. Almost every police officer killed after making multiple center-of-mass hits would not have been killed if just one of those center-of-mass shots had been a combat-effective headshot.

In the 2004 shootout between the Los Angeles Police Department and two bank robbers, the police fired about 650 rounds at the bank robbers, who were heavily armed and wearing body armor but no head protection. If the police had tried to make headshots instead of center-of-mass shots, the situation might have ended in less than 44 minutes. Even if the bank robbers were wearing ballistic helmets, it's doubtful the helmets would have protected the bridge of the nose, and some ballistic helmets do not protect the ear canal or the upper cervical spine.

DEFENSE AMMUNITION

If shot placement is good, the most essential characteristic ammunition needs is adequate penetration. If a bullet does not penetrate deeply enough to reach critical tissues, it might not cause immediate or timely incapacitation. Shot placement and penetration are more important than a bullet's ability to expand. Even a .22 short can cause immediate incapacitation if shot placement is good and the bullet has enough penetration to reach the brain stem or upper cervical spine. The belief that large-caliber handgun ammunition will knock people off their feet or that good ammunition will turn a center-of-mass hit into a one-shot stop is a myth. Large-caliber ammunition can reduce your combat effectiveness if the recoil prevents you from having good shot placement when you make follow-up shots.

Good ammunition will not compensate for bad shot placement. Disrupting the brainstem or cervical spinal cord with a bullet causes immediate incapacitation. If a bullet stops the heart, a person might be fully functional for 10 to 15 seconds. Regardless of the ammunition, a center-of-mass shot might not cause any immediate loss of function. Since jacketed hollow-point bullets might prevent over-penetration and might give you a slight advantage because of expansion, most tactical shooters use jacketed-hollow point bullets instead of ball ammunition. Based on recent military research, the belief that having a larger diameter makes a 45-caliber bullet more deadly than a 9 mm bullet is false.

Since defense ammunition is more expensive than practice ammunition, most police departments use practice ammunition when training and qualifying police officers. Most practice ammunition has less recoil than defense ammunition, and the only way to be sure that the defense ammunition you are using will not jam your gun is to run some of the defense ammunition through your gun. Jamming was less of a problem when most police officers used revolvers instead of semi-automatics.

A semi-automatic pistol may jam because of the ammunition you are using, or it may jam regardless of what kind of ammunition you use. If you are using a pistol for self-defense and cannot stop the gun from jamming, the company that manufactured the pistol might help you resolve the problem.

Before looking for a gunsmith who can stop a handgun from jamming, try different magazines and see if the gun jams when someone else shoots it. Bad magazines cause jams, and not seating a magazine correctly or having a loose grip on a gun will also cause jams. Failing to clean or lubricate a pistol may cause jamming. When you buy a new handgun, read the owner's manual before you disassemble or reassemble the pistol. New pistols tend to jam more than pistols that have cycled a hundred rounds. Most tactical shooters will not carry a pistol for self-defense until they run at least a hundred rounds through the pistol.

To understand what you can reasonably expect from a handgun bullet, you need to understand the factors that affect performance. The primary factors are penetration, permanent wound cavity, and temporary wound cavity.

Penetration

You cannot damage critical human tissues unless your bullet has enough penetration to reach these tissues. At least 12 inches of penetration in 10% ballistic (ordnance) gelatin is a good minimum standard for defense ammunition, but more than 18 inches of penetration would probably not increase combat effectiveness. You need fewer inches of penetration when shooting at the heart from the front or back than you need when shooting at the heart from the side. A bullet that enters and exits (perforates) the heart will usually cause more tissue damage than a bullet that enters (punctures) the heart but fails to exit the heart. Bullets that enter and exit are more likely to damage both walls in a heart chamber or damage several heart chambers than bullets that enter but fail to exit.

Permanent Wound Cavity

The permanent wound cavity is the cavity produced by the crushing force of a bullet as it travels through human tissue, and the size of this cavity is a good measure of how much tissue damage a bullet has caused. Increasing penetration can increase the length and volume of the permanent wound cavity.

If penetration is the same, you can increase the size of the permanent wound cavity by increasing the caliber of the bullet or by using bullets that expand as they pass through tissue. The increases in tissue damage you get from using a larger caliber bullet or a hollow-point bullet that mushrooms (expands) are hard to measure and usually less than the increases you get by increasing penetration. A bullet that tumbles or fragments might increase the side of the permanent wound cavity.

Temporary Wound Cavity

A bullet creates a temporary wound cavity when it passes through tissue. This cavity might not last for more than 5 or 10 milliseconds and decreases in size after a bullet exits the body. Hollow-point bullets lose kinetic energy faster and produce a larger temporary cavity than solid bullets, but the temporary wound cavity made by a handgun bullet is seldom large enough to cause significant tissue damage. Increasing the velocity of a bullet might not cause a significant increase in the size of a temporary cavity but may increase bullet or bone fragmentation and make nerve or muscle tissues more vulnerable to bullet or bone fragments.

HANDGUN SAFETY

Most police departments give their officers a list of firearms rules they expect them to follow, but police officers question some of these rules more than others.

Six Basic Firearms Safety Rules

(1) *Treat all guns as if they are loaded until you verify otherwise.* Accidents often occur because people verify the chamber is empty but fail to verify a magazine is empty. Do not take anyone's word that a gun is empty. Check the gun yourself. Before tactical operations, police officers might need to verify a gun is loaded.

(2) *Prevent unauthorized use of any gun you own or control.* Police at not always able to prevent the unauthorized use of their gun, and they are sometimes killed by their own gun. Firearms training should include how to protect your gun.

(3) *Always point your gun in a safe direction (control your muzzle).* Police officers sometimes point their guns at someone who might be or is a deadly threat.

(4) *Do not put your finger on the trigger until you are ready to shoot.* Police officers may put their finger on a trigger when they might need to shoot but are not ready to shoot. Even if you never intended to shoot, the fact you had your finger on the trigger when you shot might be evidence that you intended to shoot.

(5) *Consider the path your bullet may travel before you decide to shoot.* Shooting an innocent civilian or shooting another officer because of friendly fire is something that should never happen but sometimes does.

(6) *Verify your target before you pull the trigger.* Even if you verify a target to the best of your ability, mistakes happen, and these mistakes can result in criminal charges or civil lawsuits. Poor lighting makes it hard to verify a target.

Research conducted by the FBI shows keeping your finger off the trigger until you decide to shoot can increase the time it takes to shoot. According to Dr. Vincent Di Mail, who wrote <u>Gunshot Wounds,</u> keeping your finger off the trigger can increase the time it takes to shoot by about a third of a second. According to Captains Fairbairn and Sykes, who wrote <u>Shooting to Live,</u> taking longer than a third of a second to fire your first shot can get you killed. When officers qualify, they usually put their finger on the trigger before aiming and shooting.

HANDGUN SHOOTING SKILLS

Most people who have used a handgun for self-defense, such as Old West gunfighters and war veterans, realize that tactical shooting is not the same as target shooting. Most police departments do not recognize or acknowledge the difference, and the firearms training most police officers get is closer to target shooting than tactical shooting. Most police officers who complete a police academy do not shoot well enough to be considered good target shooters or good tactical shooters. The firearms training FBI and DEA agents get is superior to the training most police officers get, but police officers are more likely to face a deadly threat or get killed in the line of duty than FBI or DEA agents.

Essential skills shooting skills for a tactical shooter include:

- Know how to use a target focus during close-quarter combat.
- Know how to shoot with both eyes open during close-quarter combat.
- Know how to use a front-sight focus at distances beyond 45 feet.
- Know how to shoot with both hands or either hand.
- Know how to aim with either eye.
- Know how to shoot from behind cover.
- Know how to move and shoot at the same time.
- Know how to cant a gun and shoot over your shoulder.
- Know how to use a tactical stance.

The isosceles stance might be a good stance for target shooting, but it's one of the worst stances for tactical shooting. If you have cover, it's hard to use an isosceles stance without exposing a large part of your body. An isosceles stance might be useful if you need to shoot over your shoulders because your target is behind you. To do this, you will need to cant your handgun.

When using a tactical stance, which is similar to a boxer's stance, you can shoot from behind a vertical barrier, such as a tree, without exposing much more than your gun and one eye. Unlike target shooters who face stationary paper targets that don't shoot back, tactical shooters often face moving targets that do shoot back.

Rather than take a specific stance, a tactical shooter needs to take the best position available, which is usually a position that lets you take advantage of any cover you might have and shoot with one or both hands. Some of the positions a tactical shooter should be able to use are a prone position, crouch, kneeling position, and bladed position—which means your body is perpendicular to your target. When using an isosceles stance, your body is parallel to your target.

If your gun is already in your hand, a tactical shooter using a target focus can hit a 5-inch bullseye that's 45 feet away in less than 1.5 seconds. If your speed and accuracy are not at this level, you need to improve your reaction time or movement time to decrease your total response time. Experienced police officers usually have their guns drawn before they need them. After you master this drill, add a second shot. Allow about 2 seconds for the second shot because you will need time to recover from the recoil after the first shot.

If you face a deadly threat armed with a gun or knife, even an upper chest shot that stops the heart will give your adversary more than 10 seconds to complete the attack. Old West gunfighters avoided face-to-face gunfights because they knew the chances were good that even if they killed their adversary, they would probably be badly wounded or killed.

Old West gunfighters also realized that a fast draw did not win a gunfight if you missed, and being a good shot did not will a fight if someone fired a combat-effective shot before you had time to draw your gun. Some gunfighters would let the other person fire first if it gave them time to make an accurate, combat-effective shot or give them time to get behind cover.

The best option for a tactical shooter is to take as much time as you need to make a combat-effective, but constantly try to reduce the time it takes to make the shot. Two ways to reduce the time it takes to fire a combat-effective shot are (1) eliminate unnecessary movements and (2) make your movements smoother. Until you are combat effective when shooting slowly, do not try to shoot faster.

It might be tempting to start with a large target and change to a smaller target when your skills improve, but you cannot usually make a combat-effective shot, such as a headshot, if you cannot hit a 5-inch circle. A better option is to use a silhouette target with a 5-inch bullseye. If you miss the bullseye and hit the silhouette, you will know how far a bullet was from the bullseye.

Most silhouettes with a 5-inch gong have the gong positioned for a heart shot, but the aim point for both a heart shot and a headshot is 5 inches. You can use the square or rectangle above the gong to practice headshots, but hitting a gong and not seeing it move indicates you are using a front-sight focus instead of a target focus. At 45 feet or less, you should be able to make headshots when using a target focus. At 75 feet, you may need to use a front-sight focus when making headshots.

After you have a silhouette target with a 5-inch gong, you can add variety to your practice routine by shooting with one hand or by shooting and moving at the same time. You can also use a two-shot heart-to-head sequence. If the shot near the heart slows someone down, it might be easier to make the headshot. You can add variety by shooting one target at 21 feet, one target at 45 feet, and one target at 75 feet. When shooting at distances less than 45 feet, using a paper target, such as a 5-inch paper plate on a paper silhouette, is usually safer than using a steel target.

Stances Used for Tactical Shooting

| High Diagonal Stance | High Diagonal Stance | Low Diagonal Stance |

| Crouch | High Bladed Stance | High Bladed Stance |

High Diagonal Stance	High Diagonal Stance	Shooting Behind Back
Shooting Behind Back	Right Barricade	Left Barricade

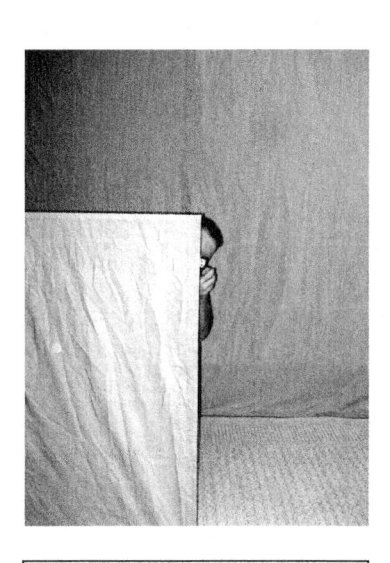

37

| High Diagonal Stance | High Diagonal Stance | Racking Slide |

| Ready Position | Low Bladed Stance | Kneeling Stance |

| Club Defense | Canted Carbine Position | Transition to Handgun |

| Knife Defense | Knife Defense | Supine Position |

Advanced Aiming Technique

Aiming aligns a gun with a target, and you can aim a gun with a front and rear sight in three different ways: focus on the target, focus on the front sight, or focus on the rear sight. Target shooters usually focus on the front sight regardless of distance, tactical shooters focus on the target during close-quarter combat, and some tactical shooters focus on the target at a distance up to about 75. It would be rare to find anyone who focuses on the rear sight when aiming a gun.

Right-handed target shooters usually use their right eye when focusing on the front sight, and right-handed tactical shooters usually use their right eye when using a target focus. Advanced tactical shooters can use either eye when using a target focus, and they can do this when both eyes are open.

Shooting with both eyes open gives tactical shooters a significant advantage when shooting at multiple targets because they can focus on a target with either eye. Whether they shoot with two hands or one hand, they use the right to focus on targets to the right and the left eye to focus on targets to the left. Right-handed tactical shooters usually focus on a target with the right eye if a target is straight ahead. If the right eye is injured, they focus on a target with the left eye.

Learning how to control which eye focuses on a target takes practice. If you want to know which eye is focusing on a target when both eyes open, point your index finger at the target and close one eye. If your index finger is focused on the target after closing one eye, the open eye is focusing on the target. If the index finger is not focused on the target after you close one eye, the eye you closed was focused on the target. Repeat this sequence until you can tell which eye is focused on a target without closing one eye.

Some people have a problem using this exercise because they get double vision and see two index fingers. If you focus on a target with your right eye and see two images of your index finger, the image to the left will be a right-eye focus. If you focus on a target with your left eye and see two images of your index finger, the image to the right will be a left-eye focus. In other words, if you see a double image, the correct image for a right-eye focus will be on the left, and the correct image for a left-eye focus will be on the right. With practice, your fingers will automatically align themselves on a target, and you will not notice a double image.

You will not see a double image when you shoot around the right side of a barricade with a right-eye focus or shoot around the left side of a barricade with a left-eye focus. You are less likely to see a double image when you point a laser pistol at a target than when you point your finger. Because of human physiology, people have a natural tendency to use a right-eye focus regardless of where a gun is pointed. If you control which eye you focus on a target, you can focus and shoot with one eye and shift your focus to the other eye as you pull the trigger.

Malfunctions

If a gun fails to fire, make sure you have a live round in the chamber, and none of the safeties are engaged. Some pistols will not fire unless a magazine is in the pistol. If you have a semiautomatic pistol, hit the bottom of the magazine to make sure the magazine is seated and rack the slide. If the magazine is empty, put a fresh magazine in the gun, hit the bottom of the magazine, and rack the slide. If a round does not enter the chamber, you might have a problem with the gun or the magazine. Locking the slide back, dropping a live round in the chamber, and releasing the slide would be a last resort. Dropping the slide on a live round may damage some pistols.

Most modern revolvers do not malfunction if correctly maintained, but older ones might malfunction by not aligning the cylinder with the barrel if the gun is fired double-action. A temporary fix for this problem is rotating the cylinder by hand until it's locked into place. Fixing this problem usually requires a gunsmith.

If a semiautomatic pistol fails to fire because a live round or casing is trapped in the ejection port, *smack*, *rack*, and *roll*. *Smack* means hit the bottom of the magazine with the palm of your support hand to make sure the magazine is seated. If your fingers are perpendicular to the barrel when you smack the magazine, it will be easy to regrip the pistol if you are using a two-hand grip. *Rack and roll* means rack the slide and rotate the gun in the direction of the ejection port at the same time. If you are right-handed, rack the slide and rotate the gun clockwise at the same time.

If an empty cartridge is sticking out the ejection port, which is called a *stovepipe*, sliding your hand back and over the ejection port may dislodge the empty casing. You can also slowly rack the slide back and tilt the pistol toward the ejection port. This movement will encourage any cartridge that gets ejected when you rack the slide to fall out of the ejection port because of gravity.

When the slide is all the way back, and the cartridge has dropped out of the ejection port, release the slide and let it move forward. Do not hold on to the slide (ride the slide) as it moves forward because this can reduce the forward momentum and cause another malfunction.

If you smack, rack, and roll, pointing your gun forward and in the direction of a potential target will decrease your response time if you need to shoot. If your target's location is unknown and you are not behind cover, try to get behind cover and scan the area for potential targets. Avoid exposing more of your body than necessary when you do the scan. If you see a potential target, change your position if it increases your cover.

A target shooter does not need to worry about cover when reloading or fixing a malfunction. Tactical shooters need to look for cover whenever they might face a deadly threat. If you do not have cover, crouching, taking a prone position, or getting into a ditch or low area might reduce your exposure to gunfire.

Multiple Targets

Most police officers are not taught how to prioritize multiple adversaries. Simplistic guidance, such as shooting the person closest to you first and never shooting anyone twice until you have shot everyone at least once, can get you killed. If you cannot avoid facing multiple adversaries by using situational awareness and recognizing danger signs, your best assets will be thinking fast, moving fast, being fast and accurate, and good luck. Staying calm, cool, and collected may also help. The five general principles that relate to multiple adversaries include:

- Make every effort possible to call for backup.
- You need 360-degree situational awareness to monitor multiple adversaries.
- Evasion or escape is usually safer than confrontation.
- Use a target focus and be prepared to shoot when you advance or retreat.
- Shoot the person who poses the most immediate deadly threat first.

Any plan for dealing with multiple adversaries is almost useless if it fails to consider incapacitation. People who recommend one shot per adversary might be correct if the shot is a headshot that causes immediate incapacitation—but three shots to the center of mass are useless if your adversary returns fire and kills you. In the 1997 North Hollywood shootout between police officers and bank robbers, unlike 650 center-of-mass shots, two headshots would have stopped the robbers.

If you make an upper chest heart shot, you can follow the heart shot with a headshot, which will cause immediate incapacitation. If you make the heart shot and miss the headshot, try again to make a headshot unless the heart shot caused incapacitation. Some adversaries will stop fighting if they get hit in the chest.

If someone you shot continues to be a deadly threat, shooting the same person again might make you an easy target for other adversaries. If you see someone aiming at you, move and shoot simultaneously and try to get behind cover. If a person you already shot is bleeding profusely and you are safely behind cover, select a different target if one is available. Severe blood loss might incapacitate the first person you shot. If your adversaries are moving, you may need to find new cover. When moving, try to keep track of your adversaries and avoid being surrounded. Always look for escape routes when you change your position.

No one can tell you precisely what you should do when dealing with multiple adversaries because success will depend partially on how quickly you adapt to a constantly changing environment and partially on luck. Mobility and deception may help you stay alive. If you're lucky, your adversaries will panic and make mistakes or flee when they see you are not an easy target.

QUICK-DRAW AND HOLSTERS

Holster designs are constantly evolving, and the number of companies that manufacture holsters is constantly increasing. Even if you know the kind of gun someone owns and what it will be used for, it's hard to predict what kind of holster the person will decide to buy. Some people buy a holster because of how it looks, and others buy a holster because of how their gun looks when it's in a holster. Most police holsters have retention devices and are not quick-draw holsters.

Being vigilant and taking your gun out of its holster when you anticipate a deadly threat is more likely to save your life than waiting until you verify a deadly and try to draw your gun fastest enough to stop the threat.

Watching body language and someone's hands may indicate it's time to take your gun out of its holster. If someone who makes a deadly threat is not armed, taking your gun out of its holster might escalate the situation. Take your gun out of its holster if you believe not taking it out will put you in a position where you won't have enough time to draw and stop a deadly attack.

A fast draw might be helpful if you get ambushed, but it might be hard to draw fast if you need to release the safety devices on your holster or have clothing covering your holster. Police holsters are usually a compromise between maximum security and maximum speed. Practice drawing from the holster you normally use.

Most of the time, a reliable draw is more important than a fast draw. Having a fast draw is less likely to save your life than having good tactical skills and good shooting skills. Good tactical skills will help you avoid being taken by surprise, and good shooting skills will help you make combative effective shots.

These observations are based on personal experience:

- It takes less time to shoot if you don't need to release a safety.
- Single action triggers take less time to pull than double-action triggers.
- Having your gun aligned on someone reduces the time it takes to shoot.
- Having your finger on the trigger reduces the time it takes to shoot.
- If a gun is holstered, you can draw faster if retention devices are already released.
- If a gun is holstered, you can draw faster if your hand is already on the grip.

Some departments do not allow their officers to use all the techniques that reduce the time it takes to fire a gun. In the 1970s, police officers used techniques that most modern police departments would never approve. Many of these techniques were taught by police instructors who had military experience before joining a police department. Elite police units, such as special response units, often use techniques that the average police officer is not trained or allowed to use.

In the Old West, having a face-to-face quick-draw gunfight was much less common than Hollywood producers would have you believe. Most gunfighters who had a fast draw preferred to ambush their adversaries or shoot them in the back because a face-to-face confrontation between two equally skilled gunfighters usually resulted in both getting wounded or killed. Most gunfighters preferred to use a shotgun or rifle against someone armed with a handgun, and shooting from behind cover was considered safer than having a face-to-face gunfight.

You do not need to be a quick-draw artist, but you should practice drawing your gun from a holster. After completing the draw, you should practice both shooting and not shooting. The reason for practicing both techniques is that automatically shooting after you draw might save your life, but a police officer is more likely to draw and not shoot than draw a shoot.

Keep your finger off the trigger when you draw until the barrel points away from your body. More than a few people have shot themselves in the leg or foot because they pulled the trigger while drawing a gun. You should also have your finger off the trigger when you reholster your gun.

When learning how to draw a gun from a holster, use an empty gun. Before each training session, make sure the chamber and magazine are empty. It's a good safety policy to have a partner when you practice drawing and shooting a gun.
As part of their training, most police officers are taught how to draw and shoot at moderate speeds.

Focus on improving safety, smoothness, reliability, and accuracy before you try to increase your speed. It will not matter how fast you can draw a gun if you cannot hit what you are aiming at after your gun clears the holster if you need to shoot. Increasing your smoothness will usually increase your speed.

If you are a tactical shooter, practice drawing your gun from the kind of holster or container—such as a purse or fanny pack—you plan to use when you carry your gun for self-defense. Two things that can help you increase the speed of your draw are good technique and frequent practice. Good technique will help you eliminate unnecessary movements that reduce your speed, and frequent practice will help you build the motor skills that make it easier for your body to move quickly.

Most right-handed people will have their holster on the right side of the body. Right-handed people might carry their gun on the left side when using a shoulder holster or a cross-draw holster. Drawing from the left side can make it easier to draw when sitting in a patrol car but harder to draw if you are in a prone position.

When deciding which holster to buy, do not forget to think about comfort. A leather holster might be softer and more comfortable than a Kydex holster, but a Kydex holster is usually more durable and less expensive than a leather holster. If you are unsure about what kind of holster you want, wearing a holster with your gun in it may help you decide. If used often, most holsters mar a gun's finish.

TACTICAL SKILLS

Tactical skills are the art and science of using your handgun correctly when facing a deadly threat. Good tactics can help you avoid potentially dangerous situations or help you deal quickly and effectively with deadly situations that you cannot avoid. You can be a good target shooter without having tactical skills.

Unlike a military situation where guns are used for killing or wounding the enemy, in a non-military situation, guns are used to stop an imminent deadly threat by causing immediate or timely incapacitation. Causing incapacitation may cause death, but the reason for using deadly force is to cause incapacitation—not death. If someone is no longer an imminent deadly threat because of incapacitation, using additional force would not be reasonable or necessary and possibly illegal.

You can resolve dangerous confrontations by using non-physical skills or physical skills. The two most common non-physical skills are (1) avoidance and (2) negotiation. *Avoidance* is recognizing and staying away from dangerous situations, and *negotiation* is the process of using verbal skills to reach an agreement that prevents anyone from being injured or killed.

Physical skills are body movements that give you a tactical advantage, such as flanking or getting behind adversaries, which will make it harder for adversaries to shoot you and easier for you to shoot them. Moving behind cover or concealment will also make it harder for adversaries to shoot you. Cover can prevent bullets from reaching you, and concealment can prevent adversaries from seeing you. Moving to a higher location can make it easier for you to see and shoot adversaries and harder for adversaries to see and shoot you. Moving and shooting at the same time will make it harder for adversaries to shoot you because most people, including most police officers, have never been trained to shoot moving targets.

Unlike target shooting, which is won or lost because of marksmanship, most deadly confrontations against someone with a gun or knife are won or lost because of what happens before you pull the trigger. Experienced police officers can often resolve a dangerous situation without firing a shot because they know how to give themselves the upper hand and leave a suspect with only two options: submit or get shot. Most people would rather submit than get shot.

As Sun Tzu explained in his classic book <u>The Art of War</u>, tactics are used to gain or maintain a position of advantage and control before and during a deadly confrontation. In most civilized countries, law-abiding citizens have a right to protect themselves when facing an imminent deadly threat, but abusing this right can have legal consequences. People with good shooting and tactical skills can often avoid the need for deadly force by maintaining a position advantage and control and de-escalating dangerous situations. Like poorly trained racecar drivers, poorly trained police officers are a danger to themselves and others.

The four elements that increase the probability of surviving a deadly threat are attitude, awareness, advantage, and accuracy. *Attitude* means you are willing to do whatever it takes to defend yourself, and *awareness* allows you to recognize, evaluate, and react to threats. *Advantage* means putting someone who is threatening you at a tactical disadvantage, and *accuracy* gives you the ability to stop a deadly threat without causing collateral damage, such as shooting an innocent person.

Decisiveness and preparation can help you survive a deadly confrontation. Decisiveness is needed to counter one of the major mistakes that can get you injured or killed: hesitation. If you do not act before it's too late, it will be too late

Preparation can help you avoid hesitation. Know in advance how you plan to act if a particular situation arises. If your department has a written use-of-force policy, which every police department should have, know what your department expects you to do when dealing with a deadly confrontation.

If departmental policy states anyone who refuses to drop a gun when ordered to do so is a deadly threat and you can respond with deadly force if other alternatives are not available, you need to evaluate the alternatives. Is it safe to use a non-lethal device, such as a Taser, after someone holding a gun has threatened to shoot you?

The legal guidelines for using deadly force are complex, and no use-of-force policy will answer all possible questions. If you have any questions about your department's use-of-force policies, get clarification from your department or speak to an attorney. Vague policies increase rather than decrease hesitation.

Progressive Levels of Awareness

- Level One—White: Maintain 360-degree situational awareness.
- Level Two—Green: Scan for danger signs.
- Level Three—Yellow: See a potential threat.
- Level four—Red: React to verified threats.

Condition white is similar to the level of awareness you should have when walking in a park. You are not expecting danger, but you need to stay alert. *Condition green* is similar to walking through the woods. Even if there are no danger signs, you realize that danger may exist, and you scan for potential threats, such as poisonous snakes. *Condition yellow* is similar to walking through the woods, seeing a poisonous snake, and watching to see what the snake does. The snake is a potential threat. *Condition red* would be seeing a poisonous snake coil up and prepare to strike. At this point, the snake is a verified threat.

Most of the time, a police officer will be at level two, which means scanning for potential threats. Seeing a potential threat will move a police officer to level 3, and reacting to the threat will move a police officer to level 4.

A problem police officers sometimes have is getting beyond level one. If you are on duty, you need to be looking for potential dangers. You will not be able to anticipate or avoid an ambush if you are not looking for situations that might be ideal for an ambush. If you don't notice that someone walking toward you is holding a knife or gun, you might be shot or stabbed while your gun is still in its holster.

Fighting to Win

Always look for a weakness in your adversary's defenses you can exploit, and doing this requires handgun skills, tactical skills, and the right attitude. The most crucial handgun skill is shooting before you get shot and making your shot combat-effective, which means your shot causes immediate or timely incapacitation. A shot that doesn't cause incapacitation is not much better than a miss.

The two most important tactical skills are recognizing and responding to danger signs quickly and correctly, which means giving yourself every possible advantage and putting your adversary at a disadvantage.

The most important attitude you need to have is a willingness to do whatever it takes to win without hesitation or regret. Shouting out profanity or threats usually indicates that you are out of control and possibly incapable of making intelligent decisions. If you cannot control yourself, you have almost no chance of controlling a dangerous situation. Based on interviews with convicted cop killers, police officers who appear to be in control of a situation are less likely to be shot than police officers who appear to be incompetent.

The famous military strategist Sun Tzu stated that a brilliant general can win without fighting. The same applies to law enforcement officers. Police officers who cannot control their fear when facing a deadly threat are a danger to themselves, fellow officers, and innocent civilians because they often use unnecessary force.

Fear is normal and uncontrolled fear is dangerous, but fear that increases your reaction times and determination can be an asset. Soldiers who can manage their fear when they feel afraid are sometimes awarded medals for acts of bravery.

Deceptions, Disruptions, and Distractions

Confusion can be effective against a deadly threat if it diverts your adversary's attention long enough for you to take appropriate action, such as shoot or get behind cover. The three techniques for causing confusion are deception, disruption, and distraction. Deceptions cause people to make bad decisions because of false information, disruptions make it hard for people to think clearly, and distractions divert people's attention from one place to another. These techniques will be more effective if you appear to be informative instead of manipulative or coercive.

Ambush

You can use concealment to stage an ambush that catches people by surprise and causes confusion. Using a distraction to divert your adversary's attention in one direction and then attack from the opposite direction can make an ambush more effective. An ambush can be very effective because it keeps an adversary from having enough time to set up a strong defense or launch a counterattack. The FBI and local law enforcement officers used an ambush to neutralize Bonnie and Clyde.

Since an ambush occurs suddenly and without provocation, awareness and prevention are the best defenses against an ambush. If you detect a potential ambush site, avoid entering the danger zone. If an ambush catches you by surprise, the options include taking cover or finding an escape route. You might be able to use suppression fire to aid your escape if an adversary is very close, but suppression fire from a handgun is unlikely to be effective against a tactical rifle at close range. Be aware that some adversaries will create points of weakness so they can funnel you into a secondary danger zone. If ambushed by someone with a sniper rifle who is more than 100 yards away, get behind reliable cover and hope for backup.

Acts of Desperation

If attacked by an adversary who wants to kill you, use every advantage you have to defeat your adversary. Be ruthless and do whatever it takes to win, such as gouging the eyes or biting the neck. A knife can be more effective than a gun at very close range if you know how to use a knife. If you win the fight and subdue your adversary, the important thing to remember is that your right to use deadly force has ended, and you are obligated to render first aid. Even if the violence you used to save your life seemed reasonable, you might face criminal charges or civil lawsuits.

Because specific techniques have been used and abused in the past, you might use one of these techniques to save your life and suffer severe consequences for using it. For example, police officers were taught to use a strangulation hold to subdue violent criminals during the 1970s. Because of complaints from the public, the same technique continued to be used, but it was called a lateral vascular neck restraint. The complaints continued, and many departments wrote policies that forbid officers from using the technique. When a situation arose where an officer used the technique to disarm someone armed with a gun, it was unclear whether police officers had a right to use a banned technique to save their lives. It might seem reasonable to believe police officers have a legal right to use wherever means are available to save their lives, but what seems reasonable might not be legal. If you have any doubts about your right to use extreme measures when defending your life, speak to an attorney.

Reality or Myth

If you have questions relating to shooting techniques or tactics, consider the source of information and whether the information is credible. The Old West gunfighter myth perpetuated by Hollywood is almost entirely myth, but Hollywood's version of the Old West has millions of viewers because it's exciting to watch. Some of the new action-adventure movies are exciting to watch, and because the produces have good technical advisers, some of the shooting techniques and tactics are better than the ones you see police officers use when their videos appear on television. It's rare to see a modern action hero use an isosceles stance instead of a tactical stance or never move and shoot at the same time.

On the other hand, Hollywood movies become amazingly unrealistic when an action hero takes on multiple adversaries armed with tactical rifles and manages to defeat all of them with a handgun. During a 1986 shootout in Florida, the FBI learned the hard way that handgun bullets are no match for high-velocity rifle bullets. Another fallacy Hollywood perpetuates is that a handgun bullet that hits the chest will cause immediate death or may knock you off your feet. You might fall if you get hit by a handgun bullet, but you will not get knocked off your feet.

Tactical Axioms

Famous military leaders, such as Sun Tze, Napolean Bonaparte, and Carl von Clausewitz, wrote military axioms that modern military leaders read and study. Some of these axions can be modified slightly and applied to law enforcement.

- Have confidence in your plan and your ability to carry out the plan.
- Try to learn your adversary's plan and try to hide your plan.
- If two plans seem to be equally effective, use the simplest one.
- Complex plans are difficult to learn, remember, and use.
- Adjust your plan to be compatible with your resources.
- Have alternative plans in case your original plan fails.
- Plan for attack and defense at the same time.
- Discontinue a plan that is not working.
- Attack when strong and retreat when weak.
- Make your enemy an easier target than you are.
- Keep your enemy off balance either by moving or by standing still.
- Take a position that makes it easy to attack, defend, or escape.
- Use a plan that benefits from your strength and your enemy's weakness.
- If your training methods are not working, change your training methods.

Whether Sun Tzu was a mythical or real person is open for debate, but the Art of War is a military classic.

Danger Signs

Look for things that might be potentially threatening. You cannot always identify criminals by how they look or dress, and some criminals are very good at not looking suspicious. Rather than judge people by how they look, judge people by how they behave. Appearances can be deceptive. Most master criminals have mastered the art of not looking like criminals.

If you investigate someone or something that looks suspicious, be in a position to defend yourself if a potential threat turns into a deadly threat. If you shoot with your right hand, carry your flashlight or clipboard in your left hand. If the threat level increases, you may want to go from having your hand on your gun to having your gun in your hand. If you need to have your gun in your hand, you probably need to advise the dispatcher of the situation or request backup.

Action and Reaction

Quickness depends on *reaction time* and *movement time*. *Reaction time* is the time it takes to scan, interpret, and react to what you see. *Movement time* is the time it takes to complete the response. The total time it takes to react and move is called *response time*. You can decrease movement time by frequently and correctly practicing a movement until it becomes automatic, and you can complete the entire movement without conscious thought. To achieve maximum speed, make the essential movements as small as possible and remove non-essential movements (*economy of movement*).

Some people have better reflexes than others because of genetics, but most people can shorten their response time by knowing what they are looking for when they scan a situation and knowing how to react because of previous training. You can shorten your movement time by practicing enough to improve muscle memory and make a movement almost automatic. Practice can also strengthen muscles and increase neuromuscular efficiency, which might increase body speed.

If you see someone start to draw a gun, and then you start to draw your gun, the action (other person drawing a gun) will usually be faster than the reaction (you drawing your gun). Action is not always faster than reaction if the size of the movement needed to complete the action is larger than the size of the movement needed to complete the reaction. If you already have a gun in your hand and someone draws a gun, the person drawing the gun might need to move the gun a greater distance before shooting than you need to move your gun before shooting. In this situation, your reaction might be faster than your adversary's action. If your gun is in your hand and you anticipate that your adversary is planning to draw, you might be able to shoot before your adversary's gun clears the holster.

Lighting

Gunfighters in the Old West took advantage of lighting by trying to have the sun at their back if they fought during the day or trying to hide in darkness if they fought at night. People who kill police officers also use darkness to gain a tactical advantage. What has changed since gunfights were fought in the Old West is the availability of flashlights that produce high-intensity light.

Most police firearms training takes place during the day, but serious crimes often occur at night. When night-vision devices are not available, using a flashlight is the best way to make a deadly threat visible in a room with little or no light. A muzzle blast can also make someone visible if a shot is fired in a dark room.

You might be able to use darkness to your advantage if your adversaries do not have night-vision devices. Police officers who work for a department that does not issue night-vision devices should consider buying a night-vision device.

To avoid detection, do not let a light source behind you silhouette your body, and do not wear something shiny that reflects light and might reveal your location. When you use a flashlight, do not let it illuminate your body. If you keep your flashlight turned on when moving through a dark area, you will reveal your location and direction of travel. If possible, get behind cover, illuminate an area long enough to check for deadly threats and see which way you want to go, and then turn the flashlight off. Try to avoid using your flashlight in the middle of an open area.

You can defend a secure area by getting behind cover and using your flashlight to illuminate a deadly funnel, such as a doorway or hallway an adversary would need to pass through to reach your position. Rather than keep your flashlight turned on, flash the area quickly and turn your flashlight off. The amount of ambient light you have and the length of the deadly tunnel will determine how often you need to flash your flashlight. If you are right-handed, flash with your left hand and hold your gun with your right hand with your finger off the trigger.

Activating a flashlight for a fraction of a second to verify a target just before you shoot is called *flash-and-shoot*. When using a gun-mounted light, you would use a short flash to illuminate the area in front of your gun, shoot if you have a target, and quickly change your location. Flash-and-shoot is not usually effective unless you use a target focus and pull the trigger when or shortly after the target is visible.

A sudden flash of bright light may cause your adversary to pause long enough for you to shoot, and some adversaries will surrender instead of risk getting shot—especially if the light temporarily blinds them.

If a gun-mounted light is on for less than a half-second, most people will not react fast enough to shoot before the light is turned off, and people who try will probably miss. If you are not behind cover, move in a lateral direction before using flash-and-shoot again. You can practice flash-and-shoot with a laser-training pistol.

Misses that Might Count

Some people say misses never count, but that's not entirely true in the real world. Misses do not count when target shooting, but they might have value in a gunfight. A missed shot may cause adversaries to run for cover, faint, flee or prematurely discharge their gun before it's aligned with your body. According to Captains Sykes and Fairbairn, who trained Shanghai Police Officers and British saboteurs, a missed shot can give you as much as a two-second advantage over your opponent. Despite the advantages you may get from missing your target, hitting aim points that damage critical tissue and cause immediate or timely incapacitation will give you more than just a two-second advantage.

If an adversary responds to a missed shot by ducking behind cover, you may be able to use suppression fire to keep the person pinned down until your backup arrives. Using suppression fire so you can advance on someone's position is a risky proposition, but criminals have used this technique to kill police officers. Having extra magazines, especially high-capacity magazines, will make using suppression fire easier. Using suppression fire increases the risk of running out of ammunition.

How to Be a Hard Target and Make Yourself Harder to Kill

Use cover or concealment whenever possible. If you need to shoot and you are not protected by cover, do not expose more of your body than necessary when you shoot, and change your position after you shoot.

Slow movements are less likely to draw attention when traveling through a dark area than fast movements. When moving through a well-light area, conceal as much of your body as possible and do not stay exposed longer than necessary.

If the chances of being discovered when crossing an open area are high, use fast, unpredictable movements to reduce of risk of getting shot, such as a zig-zag run with sharp turns. Wearing light-colored clothing or having equipment that reflects light will increase your risk of being discovered when moving through a dark area.

If you advance on people behind cover, flanking and getting behind them is usually safer than a frontal attack. If you must use a frontal attack, try to use cover as you advance and make your movements quick and unpredictable. If the distance you need to travel is very short, running in a straight line to reduce your exposure time might be safer than using a zigzag pattern.

If you work with a partner, be careful not to get in your partner's line of fire. You might be hit by friendly fire or prevent your partner from using cover fire. Working with someone you are unfamiliar with can be dangerous, especially if the person has limited shooting or tactical skills. The belief working with a partner is safer than working alone depends on who you are working with.

Mobility

Good mobility will increase your chances of winning a boxing match or a deadly confrontation. Remaining stationary makes you an easy target, and being in motion makes you a hard target. Quickly lateral movements can give you a tactical advantage when facing a gun or knife attack. If your adversary's weapon and your gun are both being held in the right hand, moving to your left will usually make it easier to avoid your adversary's weapon and protect your gun.

If you do not have someone to protect your back, look for places you can move to that will help you avoid being attacked from the rear, such as putting your back against a wall, backing into a room that you know is safe, or backing into a corner. When protecting your back, try to use an area that provides concealment or cover and has escape routes that can help you avoid being surrounded or trapped.

Whether you should shoot, shoot and move, move and shoot, or shoot while moving depends on the circumstances and your skill level. If an adversary reaches for a gun, shoot from whatever stance or place you are in if you stand a good chance of being able to neutralize the threat. This is one time when standing out in the open and shooting from a stationary position might be reasonable.

If someone is trying to shoot you, moving in a lateral direction will make you a more challenging target than moving directly at or away from the person. If you are running at or away from someone, zigzagging will usually make you a harder target than moving along a straight line, but moving along a straight line will let you cover distance faster than moving along a line that is angled or curved. Getting behind someone is usually safer than being in front of or beside someone unless the person you are standing behind is a trained tactical shooter. Most trained tactical shooters hit someone standing behind them by shooting over their shoulder.

If someone pointing a gun at you is using a two-handed grip and a front-sight focus, try to drop below the line of sight and move in a lateral direction. The time it takes your adversary to lower the gun and focus on the front sight again may give you time to fire a combat-effective shot or evade and get behind cover.

Surrendering Your Gun

Surrendering your gun is hardly ever a good option, and doing it can lead to getting killed with your own gun. Do not surrender your gun unless it gives you a tactical advantage, such as giving backup time to arrive. If your adversary is close and your gun is holstered, attempting an empty-hand gun disarm would probably be safer than surrendering your gun. If you are right-hand and you can get the barrel of your adversary's gun pointed away from your body with your left hand, an eye strike or nose punch with your right hand might be your best offensive action.

Relaxing Too Soon

Unlike target shooting, where you might be able to *call the shot* and predict where a bullet will hit, in a gunfight you might not know if or where a bullet hits until after the fight. And even if you know where a shot landed, you might not be able to tell if the bullet severely damaged critical tissues.

Profuse bleeding and visible trauma do not always indicate severe tissue damage, and police departments have documented cases where both an officer and a subject continued to fight after being hit by multiple gunshots to the torso. The exact cause for incapacitation or death might not be known until after a medical examiner completes an autopsy.

If your adversary is wearing body armor, multiple shots to the chest might not cause any significant tissue damage. Even if someone you shot in the chest at close range seems to be dead, do not assume the person is dead. Criminals often fake incapacitation or unconsciousness to gain a tactical advantage.

Even if you have control of the gun your assailant was using, your assailant might have more than one weapon. It will be hard to conduct a thorough search until your adversary is adequately restrained. In some cases, it's best to hold someone at gunpoint until backup arrives.

Use extreme caution if you need to approach a dangerous adversary and backup is unavailable. With your gun drawn, approach from a direction that makes it harder for your adversary to see you and pay attention to your adversary's hands. If your adversary cannot or will not respond to a show-me-your-hands command, look for a hand position that might conceal a weapon or make it easy for your adversary to reach for a concealed weapon.

If possible, move the adversary into a prone position and move the arms away from the body. When you move to check the hands, walk around the head, not around the feet. You might get kicked if you get too close to the feet. If the palms are not visible, lift each hand to ensure nothing dangerous is under either hand. If you are right-handed, your gun should be in your right hand, and you should search with your left hand. Keep your finger off the trigger when doing a prone body search. A sudden, non-threatening movement might cause an accidental discharge if your finger is on the trigger. After a preliminary search indicates your adversary is not armed, restrain the adversary, and conduct a more thorough search.

A common mistake is relaxing too soon after determining an adversary is not armed. Some adversaries can be a deadly threat because of strength or training when not armed. If you relax too soon after you determine someone is not armed, you might be shot by your own gun. It's best to have backup present when you restrain a dangerous adversary. If you are using handcuffs, be very careful after attaching the first handcuff. Remember to call for first aid if needed.

BUILDING SEARCHES

What we have learned after doing hundreds of building searches:

- Stop, look, and listen.
- Use your peripheral vision.
- Maintain 360-degree awareness.
- Take the less obvious route.
- Stay low and behind cover.
- Avoid large, open spaces.
- Move as quietly as possible.
- Look for potential ambush sites.
- Close or lock doors behind you.
- Use a flashlight with caution.
- Communicate with backup.
- Using a retention position when searching a building will protect your gun.

Check Your Natural Point of Aim

While holding an empty handgun in a one- or two-hand ready position, pick an aim point about ten feet away, such as a doorknob. After you pick an aim point, close your eyes and try to align your sights with the aim point. After you believe the sights are aligned, open your eyes and check the alignment. A competent tactical shooter will usually be within a few inches of the aim point.

When you do a building search, scanning the area for potential cover is just as important as scanning the area for potential threats. If you don't know where a shot came from, or you know where a shot came from but can't see the shooter, getting behind cover is usually your best option. Be aware that you might have more than one active shooter, and you need to watch for boobytraps.

Much of the active-shooter information disseminated to police officers is cosmetic at best and dangerous at worst. When police officers do a building search, they usually have little or no information about what they might find inside. When doing a building search, it's better to work with a partner than work alone if your partner is competent and you can trust your partner. When two people work together while doing a building search, one usually takes point, and the other covers the rear. If you are not part of a special unit, you will probably not have special equipment, such as body shields, suppressors, automatic weapons, or flashbang grenades.

The major challenge when entering any room is covering the blind shots until you determine if any of the blind spots are concealing a deadly threat. When dealing with low or no light situations, having a flashlight and a gun-mounted light is essential, and having night surveillance equipment would be helpful. A tactical mirror can help you look around corners.

Many of the large objects in a building, such as a desk or a file cabinet, are to some extent hollow and provide very little protection against handgun bullets and almost no protection against high-velocity rifle bullets. Most residential walls are not strong enough to stop a bullet, but a refrigerator might stop a bullet.

Communication devices can be a valuable asset when doing a building search, but be careful not to let your radio or other communication devices, such as a cell phone, disclose your location. You need to be notified by radio or other means that backup units have entered a building you are searching. Unexpectedly encountering backup units can result in friendly fire.

When doing a building search, safety is more important than speed. Most rooms have more than one blind spot, and you need to check all of them. Blind corners are typical blind spots but can also have blind spots behind furniture or drapes. If a door is closed, the entire room behind it is a blind spot.

Always scan the area you are searching for escape routes in case your find a situation that requires backup. If you decide to use a tactical retreat, try to avoid entering an area that is more dangerous than the one you are leaving and try to avoid being surrounded. Never stop looking for new escape routes.

If you are forced to retreat and one or more adversaries pursue you, setting up an ambush might be safer than continuing to run. Find a place with cover and set up an ambush. Some adversaries will surrender after they realize they were ambushed.

The following search method shows how one person can try to search a room. Methods for doing a room search with two or more people require teamwork and practice, and they are beyond the scope of this book.

Most blind spots can be exposed by changing the angle between your cover and the blind spots (*slicing the pie*). Before entering a doorway, glance as far around the left edge of the doorway as you can without exposing more than part of your head and one eye and scan the right side of the room. Move slightly to the right and scan the left side of the room the same way. Use a two-hand grip when scanning the visible corners and a one-hand grip when scanning the hidden corners.

This search method will not reveal deadly threats in the corners nearest the doorway. You might be able to check these blind shots if you use a tactical mirror to view the left and right corners, which are the corners closest to the doorway. You should not hold a tactical mirror with your gun hand. If you enter a room and realize you failed to see a deadly threat, exit the room as quickly as possible. If the room is dark, you might be able to blind your adversary with your gun-mounted light as you exit the room. If exiting the room is not a good option, try to get behind cover.

If the deadly threat you failed to discover is an imminent deadly threat, you might be able to bind your adversary with a muzzle blast. If you eliminate one imminent deadly threat, scan the room for other deadly threats as you exit the room.

When dealing with an imminent deadly threat, you might be able to use suppression fire to blind your adversary and keep your adversary pinned down while you exit the room. Another option is to drop to the ground and shoot or drop to the ground and roll and shoot. If you are in the middle of a room when you discover a deadly threat and the room has another exit, using the other exit might be an option.

A Basic Room Search

Since most police officers are lucky to have even one officer available for backup when they do a building search, one officer can use this search pattern when no other officers are available. Even if backup units are available, some departments believe that the first officer to arrive on the scene should start a building search without backup if you have an active shooter. Not having someone who can function as your rearguard will increase your risk of getting killed if an active shooter gets behind you or you have more than one active shooter.

The basic building search pattern makes two basic assumptions: one person will search the room, and the room has four corners and one entrance. The two corners farthest from the entrance are called visible corners, and the two corners closest to the entrance are called blind corners. The person shown in the graphic below is right-handed and armed with a handgun.

Diagrams one and two below show how to check the visible top corners, and diagrams three and four below show how to check the hidden bottom corners. Use a two-hand grip when checking the visible corners and a one-hand grip when checking the hidden corners. Check the hidden corners with a glance. If you have a tactical mirror, you can check the hidden corner with the mirror before you glance around the corners. When checking corners, align your gun with your line of sight. The glance can become a glace and shoot if you see an imminent deadly threat. If you do not have a rearguard, check your rear before and after each glance. When checking the hidden corners, do the first check while kneeling and the other while standing to make it hard for someone to anticipate where your head will be.

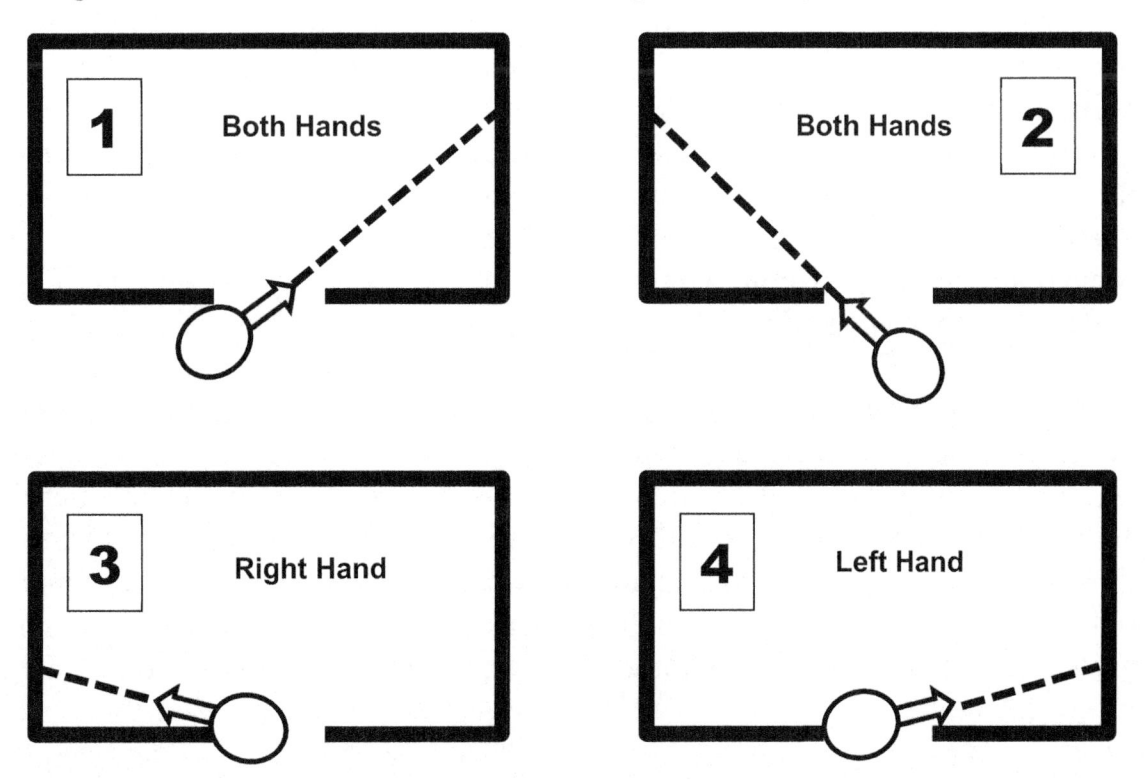

1 Both Hands

2 Both Hands

3 Right Hand

4 Left Hand

HOME SECURITY

Off-duty police officers are more likely to be attacked in their homes than they were years ago, which means home security is more important than it was years ago. In some cases, criminals burglarize or commit a home invasion robbery without realizing a police officer lives in the home.

Most states give you more latitude when defending yourself inside your home because of the Castle Doctrine or stand-your-ground laws. Having a plan in place before criminals enter or try to enter your home will reduce of risk of having anyone inside your home injured or killed. In addition to having a plan, you should also have a safe place or a safe room that will give you or your family a tactical advantage if you might have multiple intruders.

If you decide to create a safe room, find a place for the safe room that will channel intruders into your field of fire and then funnel them through a single opening (deadly funnel) before they can enter the safe room. Have something in your safe room that you and other people in the safe room can use for cover. Some of the equipment you should have in your safe room includes weapons, ammunition, communication devices, a first-aid kit, a high-intensity light, and a fire extinguisher.

If possible, your safe room should have an escape route if the intruders set your home on fire or you face overwhelming force and will not be able to defend your position. If you need to escape because your position is being overrun, a strong door with a high-quality deadbolt lock might give you extra time to retreat.

The tactical skills you use after intruders enter your home might be similar to those that you use after an ambush because ambushes and illegal entries are usually unexpected. Some illegal entries, such as a professional home-invasion robbery, are carefully planned and executed. Others, such as burglary, are often crimes of opportunity committed at random with very little planning.

Escape might be a better option than standing your ground if leaving your safe room does not increase your risk of getting injured, killed, or captured. If you decide to stand your ground, use cover and good fire discipline unless you have almost unlimited ammunition. Arming yourself with a tactical rifle or shotgun will make it easier to defend your position than arming yourself with a handgun. If intruders realize that penetrating your defenses will not be easy, they might decide to flee instead of waiting for the police to arrive. They might also realize that continuing to attack your position might get them killed.

Alarm systems or dogs can be valuable assets if they warn you that a burglary or home-invasion robbery is about to occur. Stopping intruders before they enter your home is usually safer than trying to resist after they have already entered. Shooting someone you mistakenly believed was a criminal intruder can have serious consequences. Do not use deadly force until you have positively verified your target.

Home-invasion robbers are usually more dangerous than burglars because burglars seldom take hostages and torture or kill them. One of the best ways to avoid home-invasion robberies is to keep your door locked until you verify who is at your door and what they want. If someone at your door needs to use your phone because a serious accident has just occurred, do not open the door. Tell the person to wait a minute, call the police, and tell the police about the person at your door. If the person continues to knock on your door, tell the person not to worry because you reported the accident to the police, and they should be arriving shortly.

Opening your door when you don't recognize the person knocking on your door is dangerous. Consider the possibility that the person knocking on your door wants to rob you or is distracting you so someone can illegally enter your home through a different door or through a window. Most police officers will have a gun in their hand if they open a door for someone they don't recognize.

If you are not armed and a home-invasion robber forces your door open and enters your home, exit the house as quickly as possible and go to a safe place or safe room if you have time. If you have a gun, shooting at the robber might be enough to stop the robbery, although shooting the robber might be more effective. Almost anything you do, such as grabbing a knife or an ice pick, will give you a better chance of survival than doing nothing, and it might give you enough extra time to escape.

People who plan and prepare for deadly confrontations, such as a home-invasion robbery, are more likely to survive than people who pretend nothing like this can ever happen to them. Good planning and preparation can help you stop home-invasion robberies from happening or help you survive if one does happen. Although it's secondary compared to protecting your family and yourself, good planning and preparation can also help you protect your personal property.

A good security plan for your home starts with good physical security. Most homes will not have the same security equipment that banks have, such as a walk-in vault or hold-up alarms, but just having good outside lighting, high-quality windows, and solid doors with burglar-resistant locks can be a strong deterrent to burglars and robbers. A good security system can warn you that your home might be under attack, and some of them have a panic button, which can make calling for help easier.

Knowing people are illegally entering your home does not automatically give you a legal right to stop them. If you live in a jurisdiction where the law requires that you retreat to the farthest part of your house and hide or try to escape, stopping an intruder from entering your house or searching your house for an intruder might be against the law. Speak to an attorney if you are uncertain about your legal rights if some breaks into your home.

Even if you have a legal right to search for intruders, it's safer to let a team of police officers search. Whether you are a police officer or a civilian, do not have a gun or any other weapon in your hand when the police arrive.

STREET CONFRONTATIONS

A *street confrontation* is when you face a threat because you are walking along a street or through an open area such as a parking lot. Having a gun will not guarantee your safety, but it will give you more control over your safety than agreeing to do whatever a criminal demands. Submission might be effective if a criminal's primary goal is to steal your valuables and flee, but if a criminal tries to force you into a vehicle, resistance will probably be a better option than compliance. Rape victims are often tortured and or killed after being abducted.

A gun is not the only weapon people can use for self-defense, but it's usually the most effective weapon. Some criminals might be deterred by wasp or pepper spray, but others might become more violent after you spray them with chemicals, and you might be blinded by the chemicals you use against criminals. The martial arts techniques most people learn will not be effective against physically superior criminals who are good street fighters or criminals who are high on drugs. The defensive tactics training most police officers get now is less effective than it was in the 1970s because police departments no longer teach the most effective techniques.

Street safety starts by recognizing some basic principles:

- Money or expensive items, such as jewelry, will attract criminals.
- Violent crimes are easier to commit in dark or secluded areas.
- Avoid areas that make it easy for people to approach you without being seen.
- Walking too close to a blind corner can leave you vulnerable to attack.
- Seek help or try to flee if you believe you are being followed.
- Be suspicious if people hide one or both hands or cover their faces.
- Be cautious when strangers approach and offer or ask for favors.
- Do not talk with strangers who are in vehicles or near alleys.
- Any stranger who refuses to take *no* for an answer is a potential threat.
- Reposition yourself if people try to surround or get behind you.
- Try to look inside a room for signs of danger before you enter.
- After you are in a room, try to watch the doors and other entrances.
- Traveling in a group is usually safer than traveling alone.
- A stranger who tries to force you into a vehicle is a deadly threat.
- Most criminals prefer to attack people who look like easy victims.
- Be very cautious when entering or leaving your home or place of business.
- Unusual or unexpected people or things should raise your level of awareness.
- Trust your instincts and try to avoid situations that make you feel apprehensive.

The value some of these principles have will depend on the situation. Open spaces can help you maintain a greater distance between you and potential threats, but they can also make you more visible. For example, walking in the street might help you avoid walking close to people you believe might be dangerous, but it can also make you more visible to people looking up or down the street. If you see a potentially dangerous situation in front of you, turning around and going back in the direction you came from might be your best option. Taking a longer route and being late is better than being attacked because you took a shorter route.

Unless you are willing to throw fate to the wind, walking in areas that make it easy for someone to approach you and are known to be high-crime areas should be avoided. If you are walking one of these places, constantly scan the area for potential or actual threats and take evasive action if you see either one.

Well-lit areas with high levels of pedestrian traffic and police or camera surveillance are not the kind of places most criminals would pick if they wanted to commit a crime. On the contrary, most criminals prefer to commit crimes in places where easy detection of their crimes is not possible. Unfortunately for private citizens, this is not always the case. Some criminals commit violent crimes in front of multiple witnesses to impress friends or intimidate other gangs.

As stated earlier, you have four levels of awareness.

- Level One—White: Maintain 360-degree situational awareness.
- Level Two—Green: Scan for danger signs.
- Level Three—Yellow: See a potential threat.
- Level four—Red: React to verified threats.

Before entering a large, dark parking garage at night, level-one awareness is probably sufficient. After you enter the parking garage, go to level-two awareness and scan for danger signs, such as two or three people hanging around a parked car for no apparent reason. If you walk past these people and after you walk by you, notice that they might be following you, go to level-three awareness because you might be facing a potential threat. If you take your keys out to unlock your car door and they try to surround you, go to level-four awareness because the situation indicates you have a verified threat, and it's time to react.

If an uninvited person or a group of uninvited people try to enter your car, the crimes you might be facing include carjacking, kidnapping, rape, torture, or murder. Trying to open your car door might be an innocent mistake, but forcing your car door open or breaking a window to gain entry indicates you might be facing a deadly threat. If someone breaks one of your car windows and runs away, you are probably not facing a deadly threat. If you have questions about your legal rights when facing a deadly threat or using any of the following options, speak to an attorney.

Your first option would be to throw your car keys away and run for the nearest exit. If the criminals ignore your car key and try to catch you, the crime they want to commit is probably more serious than a carjacking. If the only crime they wanted to commit was a carjacking, the criminals would probably recover your car keys and steal your car—but they would not try to stop you from escaping.

If the criminals prevent you from escaping, you are probably facing a deadly threat if they surround you and try to restrict your movements. If you have a way to escape, escape will still be your best option. You might be able to escape if you blind your adversaries with a strong chemical spray.

To believe help will run to your rescue if you scream or blow a police whistle might be overly optimistic. You might be lucky, and someone capable of helping you might respond, but you also read stories about girls being raped in a public place, and none of the people who witnessed the rape called the police.

If no one comes to your aid, you need to decide how far you are willing to go to stop the attack or give yourself a chance to escape. Some "experts" recommend taking a knife out of your purse and threatening to cut or stab your attackers if they don't let you go. If your attackers are hardened criminals, they will probably not take your threat seriously because they doubt that you have the experience or will to carry out a successful knife attack.

If you have a knife and you are willing and able to use it, don't use the knife as a threat. Keep the knife concealed until you have a chance to cut or stab one of your attackers and then try to escape. If one of the attackers is disabled because of a cut or stab wound, the attackers might decide that it's better to flee than wait for the police to arrive. If the police capture the wounded attacker, most criminals realize that the police will probably get the names of the other attackers.

If this were a Hollywood movie, the victim would probably shoot all the attackers with a concealed handgun, and all the attackers would immediately drop to the floor. Unless all the shots were headshots, most or none of the attackers would drop to the floor, and all or most of the attackers would be capable of subduing the victim. Based on tactical anatomy, only a headshot causes immediate incapacitation. A heart shot seldom causes immediate incapacitation, and multiple center-of-mass shots might not cause any incapacitation. If the victim is armed with a handgun and willing and able to use it, the best option is usually to fire one or more shots at the attackers and try to escape and fire additional shots if the attackers pursue. Once again, if you have any questions about the legality, speak to an attorney.

Even if you shoot one or more attackers, one or more attackers may pursue and try to recapture you before you reach safety. If you decide to take shots at the attackers pursuing you, try to get behind cover before you shoot. The attackers might also be armed with guns. If you can get behind cover when the attackers cannot see you, you might be able to ambush your attackers.

Parking garages tend to be more dangerous than grocery store parking lots because many of the crimes that occur in parking lots are larcenies instead of violent felonies, such as breaking into unoccupied vehicles. When violent crimes occur in parking lots, they often occur when someone exits or enters a vehicle. People who exit or enter vehicles are more likely to be thinking about what they need to do next than notice what's happening around them.

Before you exit a vehicle, scan the immediate area for potential threats. Criminals planning a rape, abduction, or carjacking will wander around a parking lot until they see a potential target and then approach the target. If you see a potential threat approaching your vehicle, stay in your vehicle and keep your doors locked. If someone approaches your vehicle, taps on your windows, and motions you to roll your window down, look directly at the person and shake your head no. If the person does not leave, honking your horn to draw attention to your vehicle or picking up your cell phone and calling the police may encourage your visitor to leave.

If the person does not leave, start your engine and be prepared to leave the parking space if the person attempts to break one of your windows or force your door open. The person on the driver's side of your vehicle may try to distract you while an accomplice tries to force entry on the other side of your vehicle. At this point, your best option will usually be honking your horn as you pull out of the parking space. Drive to a safe place and report the incident to the police.

Ignore any inclination you have to draw your gun and shoot someone you believe might be trying to break into your vehicle. You might be wrong about why someone is banging on your window—the person might be trying to tell you that you have a flat tire—or the person might be trying to break your window. If a person breaks into your vehicle and tries to grab you, using a gun for self-defense might be reasonable or necessary but might not be legal. An attorney might be able to tell you if you have a right to use deadly force when someone pulls you out of your vehicle.

Entering a vehicle can be just as dangerous as exiting a vehicle. If you open a door or a truck to load packages, stay alert to what's happening around you. If you open a door, criminals might force you into your vehicle and rob, rape, or abduct you. If someone is trying to force you into a vehicle, use any technique or weapon you have available to escape. Possible techniques include screaming, biting, or gouging eyes, and possible weapons include using a gun, knife, or chemical spray. If a criminal drives away with you in your vehicle, your chances of being rescued before you are raped, tortured, or killed and not very good. If you are kidnapped and held for ransom, your chances of being returned alive are not very good if you can identify the kidnappers. Violence used to resist abduction is *usually* legal.

If you open a door and believe someone approaching you is a threat, lock the door and move away from your vehicle. If the person pursues you, move away as fast as possible, call for help if possible, and resist abduction.

Some criminals will use friendly conversation to gain your trust and make you an easier target. If a criminal decides pleasant conversation will not work but still want to commit a crime, friendliness may turn into anger or aggressiveness. If you are having a conversation with this kind of person, make it clear that you are looking at the person to the extent that you will be able to describe or identify the person if necessary. Failing to make eye contact with this kind of person might be interpreted as a sign of weakness and encourage a criminal to be even more aggressive. If a criminal's verbal threats turn into physical violence, use reasonable and necessary self-defense methods to protect yourself. Escape is almost always a better option than using potentially lethal force. If you are lucky, someone might try to assist you, and the criminal might decide that it's better to flee than fight.

This advice applies to police officers. If you believe you are facing a deadly threat, you might be able to draw your gun and conceal it behind your back without escalating a potentially violent situation. While your gun is concealed, listen to what someone says and decide if the person is a deadly threat. People can sound irrational or angry and not be dangerous. In some cases, listening to what a person says and remaining calm will deescalate a situation faster than threats and a show of force. Remaining calm will help police officers make rational decisions and have better control over their body movements. Using deadly force should be a last resort.

Whether you are a police officer or a private citizen, you need to be familiar with behaviors that indicate someone is lying.

Indications of Deception

- Abnormal body movements: constantly moving or changing postures.
- Changes in breathing: rapid or deep breathing or holding your breath.
- Changes in complexion: complexion may become flushed or blanched.
- Voice changes: the voice cracks or the pitch gets higher.
- Dryness of mouth: asking for something to drink or licking the lips.
- Answers or statements are evasive, vague, or contradictory.
- Excessive perspiration: may affect the axilla (armpit), hands, or face.
- Excessive swallowing: may be indicated by the movement of the larynx.
- Fidgeting: constantly touching or rubbing the face or hands.
- Head, neck, or shoulder movements that are stiff or mechanical.
- Nervous responses: inappropriate emotions, words, or hesitations.
- Rapid eye movement: moving eyes quickly or looking around.
- Restlessness: tapping fingers, clenching hands, or chewing lips or nails.
- Words or hand gestures are incomplete, vague, or meaningless.
- Gestures or facial expressions are inconsistent with spoken words.

While there is no way to guarantee you will always know if someone is lying, you can improve your chances of knowing you are being lied to by recognizing the signs of deception. Indications of lying are usually caused by emotional changes that occur because of guilt, and some criminals do not feel any guilt when they lie. It also appears the ability to lie without being detected improves with practice.

If people believe they are doing a good job deceiving you, they often get careless and make statements you know or can easily prove are false. Even if you cannot prove someone is lying, just believing someone may be lying should elevate your level of awareness. Rather than accuse people the instant they say something you believe is false, it is usually better not to mention your suspicions and let them continue talking. Give them enough rope, and they might hand themselves.

Refusing to look someone in the eye is often mentioned as an indication that someone is lying, but criminals are often very good at lying and looking you directly in the eye at the same time. If they are lying to you while looking you in the eye and you look away, this might be considered a sign of weakness and might encourage criminals to lie even more. Be very suspicious of people who look you in the eye and tell you they never lie or tell you how religious they are.

Historically, criminals who specialize in con games seldom use physical violence, but violent criminals, such as robbers and rapists, sometimes use the same kind of deceptions that a con artist uses to swindle victims:

- Appear to be friendly, harmless, or helpless.
- Ask for information or help.
- Offer a gift or favor to build a friendship.
- Pose as someone you can trust.
- Use conspicuous honesty to build trust.
- Suggest an easy way to make or save money.
- Tell you how lucky you are to know them.

Rather than refuse to answer a question, a con artist may answer part of the question, answer a different question, or try to divert your attention by asking you a question.

To counter these deceptions, do not make impulsive decisions, beware of strangers who offer something free, and avoid people who become overly friendly. Be very cautious of people who ask you to go with them or encourage you to get out of your car. Be especially vigilant if a stranger starts a conversation and while the two of you are speaking, another stranger unexpectedly appears and tries to join the conversation. Con artists often work as a team, and one team member will usually pretend to be on your side. Con artists and television advertisers often use the same technique. They make vague statements about what might be true, but they never offer any evidence or proof that what they say is true. For example, you should do what I say or buy what I'm selling because fortune favors the bold. Being cautious is more likely to make you wealthy or keep you alive than being bold.

TACTICAL TRAINING PROTOCOLS

Being able to draw, aim, and shoot a handgun without consciously thinking about the movements is called *unconscious competence*. After you start the draw, your body will automatically perform all of the movements without additional thought unless something occurs that causes your brain to change from automatic behavior to conscious behavior, such as having someone surrender. Unconscious competence is the best type of competence to have during a deadly confrontation. After you decide to shoot, you can stop thinking and start shooting.

If you know what skills and level of competence you want to achieve, you can shorten the training time by setting goals. The most effective goals have elements represented by the acronym *SATISFY*.

S-Specific: Set goals that are clearly defined, measurable, and essential.
A-Achievable: Do not set goals that are beyond your ability to achieve.
T-Timely: Set goals that help you learn the essential skills at the right time.
I-In writing: Write your goals down and record your progress.
S-Simple: Make your goals easy to understand and easy to visualize.
F-Flexible: Modify your practice to improve your areas of weakness.
Y-You are responsible: Achieving your goals is your responsibility.

The goals for a tactical shooter include accuracy, speed, shot placement, and tactical skills. The accuracy you need to be combat-effective will not make you a champion target shooter, but it will help you survive a gunfight. For a tactical shooter, tactical skills are usually more critical than handgun skills.

Tactical anatomy is not essential for target shooters because points are seldom scored because of any direct relationship between hits and the location of critical tissues. Even if the size of an X-ring and a tactical aim point are similar, tactical shooters do not get extra points for shooting the smallest group. Any shot within the circumference of the aim point will be combat effective.t visualize human organs when shooting at the X-ring. To make tactical training realistic, tactical shooters need to visualize they are hitting aim points, not scoring competition points.

Tactical firearms training will not be effective unless it gives you the skills you need to survive deadly confrontations, and practice will not be effective unless it helps you improve or maintain these skills. If your competence is measured by your ability to shoot stationary targets while using a front sight focus, and you get credit for hitting areas of a target that are unlikely to cause incapacitation because they are not based on tactical anatomy, you are training to be a target shooter, not a tactical shooter. Most police training will not even make you a good target shooter.

Police departments that offer unrealistic training should not be surprised to hear that there is no correlation between high qualification scores and low hit rates when officers shoot at criminals. During close-quarter combat, officers are more likely to use a target focus than a front-sight focus, which means using a shooting method they were not trained to use.

Depending on the quality of your practice, one hour of practice can be an hour well spent or an hour wasted. Regardless of how many hours you practice, high-quality practice usually produces high-quality results, and poor-quality practice usually produces no results or poor-quality results.

You often see high-quality firearms instructors offer low-quality firearms training because of departmental policies or because the minimum state standards for qualification are extremely low. Many of these instructors would never use the techniques they teach in class if they were involved in a deadly confrontation, but these are the techniques the department or state requires them to teach to avoid losing their firearms teaching certification.

Listed below are recommendations that can improve firearms training.

Prioritize: Emphasize and teach practical shooting skills.
Explain: Describe the shooting skills being taught and provide instruction.
Demonstrate: Show students what it looks like to perform the skill.
Supervise: Detect, explain, and correct the mistakes a student makes.
Motivate: Encourage effort, patience, and perseverance.
Confirm: Compliment students who perform a shooting skill correctly.

Two areas where police programs often fall short are *content* and *repetition*. Even if police officers were taught tactical shooting skills that helped them survive deadly confrontations, most departments do not give their officers enough time to master, maintain, or improve tactical shooting skills. After several years, most police officers will not be able to target shoot as well as they did when they graduated from the academy. If practicing football or baseball once a year would not help you maintain or improve your football or baseball skills, why would anyone believe that shooting once a year will help you maintain or improve your shooting skills?

Reality-based training is a popular concept in law-enforcement circles, and most departments agree that officers should be given realistic training. If this is what they believe, it's hard to understand why national statistics and police reports show that most police firearms training is unrealistic. If realistic training is a fundamental goal, state regulatory agencies and police departments can require or implement changes to make police firearms training more realistic. Until some changes are made, police hit rates will continue to be about 30% or lower.

- General Julian S. Hatcher
- Captain William E. Fairbairn
- Captain E. A. Sykes
- Colonel Rex Applegate
- Colonel Jeff Cooper
- Colonel Charles Askins
- Border Patrol Agent Bill Jordan
- Officer Jim Cirillo

Although some of these eight men were exceptional target shooters, they all recognized that a gunfight is much more than a shooting match. It's not easy to understand why some people believe or say they believe a gunfight is a shooting match. Some of the experts listed above have suggested a lack of combat experience, political correctness, a financial interest in target shooting, or poor judgment might be the cause. Colonel Rex Applegate stated you cannot adapt the sport of target shooting to the realities of combat, and a few legendary competition shooters have openly stated even practical pistol shooting is a shooting sport.

Tactical shooting is a serious business, and this book has tried to present factual information that will give tactical shooters a better chance of surviving deadly confrontations. Tactical shooting is not target shooting.

Reality-based training concepts are often used when teaching first-aid but seldom used when teaching police officers how to shoot. If police departments applied reality-based training concepts such as *goal analysis*, *instructional objectives*, *performance analysis*, and *measurable objectives* to firearms training, they would not have police officers standing out in the open shooting stationary paper targets at the target's center of mass.

If you apply goal analysis to tactical shooting, you need to start by focusing on speed, accuracy, and shot placement. Being fast will be meaningless if you miss, and moving slowly to improve your accuracy will be meaningless if you get killed before you have time to fire a shot. Since the goal is to fire the first combat-effective shot, you need to increase your speed and accuracy at the same time until you can fire a combat-effective shot in less time. You can analyze your performance by using a timer and seeing if you can reduce the time it takes to fire a combat-effective shot. Your two measurable objectives would be the time shown on the timer, and whether you hit the aim point you were shooting at. The aim point for a headshot and a heart shot is 5 inches.

When training a tactical shooter, your primary instructional objective is to keep police officers alive when facing a deadly threat. If you are going to keep police officers alive when facing a deadly threat, you need to anticipate what kind of weapon might be used and the combat environment. At minimum, you need to teach police officers how to protect themselves against a gun or knife attack and how to deal with no light or no light conditions when searching a building.

Practical Shooting

Unlike soldiers who shoot to kill and law enforcement officers who shoot to incapacitate, practical shooters shoot to win competitions, which is why practical shooting is a shooting sport. On the other hand, the fact that practical shooting is a shooting sport does not mean a tactical shooter would not benefit from using some of the skills a practical shooter uses to win competitions. Practical shooters learn critical shooting skills that police officers should but don't learn, such as shooting while moving, shooting moving targets, and shooting from awkward positions.

If the average practical shooter and the average police officer used the same qualification course that police officers use, practical shooters would almost always get higher scores than police officers. The average practical shooter practices shooting more than the average police officer, and practical shooting courses are more realistic than the courses police officers use when they train or qualify. Practical shooters are constantly trying to increase their speed and accuracy, whereas most police officers are satisfied with their shooting skills if they qualify every year.

Instead of following a military training principle that states train the way you fight and fight the way you train, most police departments follow a training principle that states train to qualify—no more or no less. Two other areas where practical-shooter training is better than most police firearms training are target acquisition and target discrimination. Practical shooters try to increase their ability to acquire targets quickly and discriminate between acceptable and unacceptable targets. If you arrive on an active shooter scene with two active shooters, you need to acquire your targets quickly and discriminate between the active shooters and innocent students.

When police officers qualify, you sometimes see them put a colored sticker on their target to avoid shooting at someone else's target, and you might find extra holes in your target because someone else shot holes in your target. Rapid target acquisition and target discrimination should be part of a police firearms program.

Police qualifications should be more than a once-a-year chance to practice or demonstrate your firearms skills; they should also include training that might help police officers improve their shooting skills. A review of the FBI's Officers Killed in the Line of Duty statics would be a good starting point for new training material. If police officers have been killed by gun or knife attacks, firearms instructors could show officers what they might be able to do to avoid getting killed under similar circumstances. After the FBI shootout in 1986, the FBI did a comprehensive review of what went wrong and changed policies and training.

One thing you will seldom see a police officer or practical shooter do is fire a shot and then immediately look over your shoulder. What often separates a police target shooter or a practical shooter from a tactical shooter is a total disregard for what's happening behind you. Ignoring what's behind you can get you killed.

Dry-Fire Practice and Laser Practice

Dry-fire practice is the process of aiming and pulling the trigger when a gun is empty. Pulling the trigger without disrupting the barrel-target alignment indicates trigger control. Because you are not using live ammunition, dry-fire practice reduces training costs, and it's safe if the gun is not loaded. Before dry-firing a handgun, check with the company that manufactures the gun to make sure dry-firing the gun will not damage any part of the gun, such as the firing pin.

Frequently dry firing some handguns may decrease their reliability. Using a snap-cap when you dry fire a gun might reduce the risk of damaging your handgun. If you are using a 1911-series handgun of a Glock, racking the slide on an empty chamber or dropping the slide on a cartridge in the chamber may damage the pistol.

A training pistol that fires a laser beam instead of a live round can be a good tool for training a tactical shooter if you use the training pistol the same way a tactical shooter would use a combat handgun. Instead of using a laser pistol to improve your ability to focus on the front sight, use it to improve your ability to use a target focus. Practicing your draw with a laser pistol is safer than practicing your draw with live ammunition and less expensive. If you have a gun-mounted light on a laser training pistol, you can practice flash-and-shoot techniques and building searches. Using a laser training pistol is also an excellent way to practice shooting while moving.

Practicing with a laser-training pistol is more expensive than dry-fire practice because you need to buy a laser pistol. High-quality laser training pistols are expensive and not always reliable. Most high-quality laser-training pistols look and feel like tactical handguns. Before you buy a laser-training pistol, find out what kind of warranty comes with the pistol, how much it will cost to repair the pistol after the warrant runs out, and how long it will take to repair the pistol.

Most hand lasers come with a warning that you should not shoot someone in the eye with a laser beam, but some of the companies that produce these devices do not seem to believe that shooting someone in the eye is dangerous. If you have any concerns about safety after you read the instructions that come with a laser-training pistol, contact the company that manufactures the laser pistol for clarification.

Most of the early laser-training devices used a red laser beam, but some of the newer ones come with a green laser beam. Green laser beams are usually more visible during the day than red laser beams, but red laser beams are highly visible at night when using red reflectors as targets. For practice to be realistic, a laser-training pistol should not fire a continuous laser beam when you hold the trigger down. When you pull the trigger, the beam should be on just long enough for you to see what you hit. Your laser-training pistol should have adjustable sights if you want to use a front-sight focus when shooting a 5-inch target at 75 feet. A laser-training pistol is not a substitute for live-fire exercises.

Non-Lethal Handguns

Most Airsoft spring-powered pistols are suitable for practicing at close range, and these replica pistols are inexpensive and realistic. Airsoft handguns are considered non-lethal (about 300 fps), but this does not mean they are incapable of causing injuries. Any bad habits you develop because of incorrectly using a non-lethal handgun might be repeated when using a lethal handgun.

Force-on-force training is purposely shooting a non-lethal gun at a person to improve your handgun or tactical skills. Any time you are doing force-on-force training with a non-lethal handgun, wear appropriate safety equipment and verify that everyone you are practicing with is also wearing the required safety equipment.

Paintball guns are potentially more dangerous than Airsoft guns, but they are generally safe to use if you wear appropriate safety equipment and follow the safety procedures that apply to paintball guns, which are also called *markers*. Barrel plugs that prevent paintballs from exiting the barrel should not be removed until everyone is wearing eye protection and other required safety equipment. Before you start force-on-force training, test the muzzle velocity of a marker with a chronograph to make sure the velocity of the paintballs is not more than 300 fps. Never remove eye protection until the practice exercise is entirely over. Head, face, and neck protection (neck guard) should be required until all markers have barrel plugs.

If you are doing force-on-force training, the number of paintballs a shooter carries should be the same as the number of bullets the shooter carries on duty. A hit that completely misses standard aim points should not be counted as a hit. Since a bullet that hits a leg will not stop someone from returning fire and killing you, do not count a paintball that hits a leg unless you are defending against a knife attack. Any shot that hits the head should be counted as a hit even if it misses the 5-inch aim point. If you count poorly placed shots during force-on-force training, you are not training people to use correct shot placement during a deadly confrontation.

A *break* is a paint mark a paintball leaves after impact. Marks less than the size of a quarter might not be from a direct hit, and they should not be counted. For paintball practice to be useful, the settings and scenarios should be realistic and not designed for entertainment. Paintball force-on-force practice can be one-on-one, team-against-team, or one or two players against a team.

Replica air pistols that shoot pellets or BBs are realistic, inexpensive to shoot, and accurate, but they should not be considered non-lethal weapons, and they should be treated the same way you treat a handgun that shoots regular bullets. The pellets or BBs from an air gun usually have less range and penetration than bullets propelled by gunpowder, but they may cause serious injuries, such as blindness or death. The maximum velocity for an air rifle is about 1100 fps, but the velocity for most air pistols is 350 to 600 fps.

Ricochet

A ricochet is a rebound that occurs if a bullet bounces off a surface. Factors that affect ricochets are the shape, velocity, and composition of a bullet, the nature of the surface a bullet hits, and the angle of incidence, which is the angle between the bullet's path and the surface a bullet hits. A bullet that hits a heavy, stationary metal target is more likely to rebound and hit the shooter than a bullet that hits a lightweight, swinging target. A swinging target is sometimes called a reactive target because it moves when you hit it.

The reactive targets that shooters use come in various sizes and shapes. Most tactical shooters use steel silhouettes with or without a gong. A gong is usually a circular piece of steel that swings when hit by a bullet. The perfect combination for a tactical shooter would be a silhouette with a 5-inch gong for headshots and a 5-inch gong for heart shots. Never use a metal target at less than the minimum safe distance recommended by the manufacturer.

Paper targets do not cause ricochets, but the metal frames used to hold them may cause a ricochet. You can avoid this problem by using wooden or plastic frames to mount paper targets, or you can mount paper targets on a cardboard box. Paper pie plates stapled on a wooden stick are good targets for practicing tactical shooting at close range, and a balloon filled with helium and tied to a string can give you practice shooting at a moving target. Plastic or rubber balls that hang on a string or are rolled across the ground can also be used as moving targets.

Ricochets have limited tactical value because it's hard to predict where a bullet will go after a ricochet. If you use the wrong angle of incidence, the ricochet angle may be too high or too low, and if the surface you hit is uneven, the bullet may move in a lateral direction. Hitting a hard (unyielding) surface tends to give you a lower ricochet angle than hitting a soft (yielding) surface.

Some studies indicate you can shoot a bullet along a hard, smooth wall at an angle smaller than 45 degrees, and the bullet may flatten and travel between 1 and 8 inches off the wall. Even though the path of a bullet that ricochets off a wall is hard to predict, firing multiple shots or using a shotgun instead of a handgun may increase your chances of hitting someone who is walking close to a wall.

Bullets that hit wooden siding, plaster walls, thin metal, or typical window glass are more likely to penetrate than ricochet. If a bullet penetrates a windshield, the glass will usually deflect the bullet up or down.

Some frangible bullets are considered safe when using reactive metal targets at close range because they disintegrate upon impact and do not contain lead. Even though frangible can make shooting reactive targets at close range safer, shooting someone with a frangible bullet can result in serious injuries or death. Frangible bullets might be used in a tactical situation that requires limited penetration.

Mental Practice

Scientific studies have shown that some athletes benefit from mental practice as they do from physical practice. Mental practice is very effective because the changes in the brain after mental practice are like those that occur after physical practice. Both types of practice can improve motor skills, and mental practice does not limit the training scenarios you can create.

Creating a what-if scenario with correct shot placement is an excellent way to use mental practice. Some studies have found that mental practice is most effective when used with physical practice. If you are a tactical shooter, you can mentally create imaginary targets and keep both eyes open when you shoot at the targets.

For mental practice to be effective: (1) the learner must be relaxed, (2) the mental images must be sharp and clear, and (3) the learner must understand what the goals are and what needs to be done to achieve these goals. In addition to tactical skills, mental practice can include attitudes, emotions, and vocalizations because adding extra details will make your mental practice more realistic.

Many people do not understand your brain is your most important weapon, and there is much more to a gunfight than just a shooting match because using your brain can give you the tactical advantages you need to win a gunfight. Mental practice gives you the ability to practice gunfights in your mind and learn from your mistakes without having to suffer the fatal consequences that might have occurred if you made similar mistakes in a real gunfight. To paraphrase an old Samurai maxim: Tomorrow's fights can be won during today's mental practice.

Most scenarios are created by using *what-if* scenarios that relate to a specific activity, such as a building search or a gunfight involving multiple adversaries. You can mentally change the characteristics of the building you are searching or mentally change the number or location of your adversaries.

Even Brian Enos, a legendary competition shooter who was shooting about 25,000 rounds per year, used mental practice to improve his shooting skills. Most of his visualizations and mental rehearsals involved interactions with targets more than interactions with human adversaries. The fact that someone with extraordinary shooting skills was using mental practice to improve his marksmanship is a strong indication that Brian Enos believed mental practice was beneficial.

If you get good at using mental practice, you may be able to stay calm but feel your respiration or pulse rate increase when you enter a stressful part of one of your imaginary scenarios. The first time you try mental practice, go straight through a new scenario without stopping to correct mistakes. After becoming more familiar with a new scenario, stop and repeat the parts of the scenario that cause you problems. Using mental practice is a good way to build speed and self-confidence. Rather than repeat scenarios you have already mastered, create new scenarios.

Handling Stress and Panic

The best way to counteract panic is to give people realistic training that improves their chances of surviving a deadly confrontation. It's easy to understand why people who try to use a front-sight focus panic when someone is shooting at them, and they have a hard time focusing on the front sight instead of looking at the someone who is trying to shoot them. Not only is it normal for people to look at someone who is trying to kill them instead of focusing on the front sight, but also poor lighting can make it hard to see your front sight. It's also hard to focus on your front sight when the person trying to kill you keeps moving, and you cannot keep your front over a moving target long enough to focus on the front sight.

Some people believe panic is normal. You should adjust your shooting so you can work around disruptive psychological reactions such as panic by doing things such as convulsively gripping your gun or pulling the trigger by squeezing the grips with all four fingers simultaneously. It's doubtful the people who recommend or teach these techniques have ever used them themselves during a gunfight because using them will tighten your muscles and slow your movement when you need to be fast and flexible. A vice-like grip on a gun will also cause muscle fatigue and cause your arm to shake. To maintain speed and accuracy, your grip needs to be firm but not tight, and your body needs to be flexible, not rigid.

The same people who recommend extreme muscle tension as a remedy for panic are often the same people who tell tactical shooters they should almost always use a front-sight focus. If you are in a state of panic that forces you to maintain a death grip on your gun and make a tight fist to pull the trigger, you are not likely to have the fine motor skills that are needed to use a front-sight focus because the excessive muscle tension will cause shaking and make it hard to keep a gun steady.

Anyone who has ever worked with a group of well-trained tactical shooters knows that all of them are not equally brave, and most of them have no desire to be heroes, but when the chips are down, all of them will do what it takes to get the job done. Despite signs of stress, such as profuse sweating, they do what they were trained to do and remain functional if what they were trained to do appears to be working. You might see people panic when they discover their training or equipment is useless and have no idea what to do next.

If your training and equipment are good and you have confidence in your training and equipment, you are less likely to have extreme psychological reactions, such as paralyzing fear or panic, when facing a deadly threat. Perfect practice does not always produce perfect results, but imperfect practice usually produces imperfect results. Using a front-sight focus during close-quarter combat is a perfect example of imperfect training. Whether you are a soldier or a law enforcement officer, no training, bad training, or insufficient training can get you killed.

Low-Light and No-Light Practice

A large percentage of all deadly confrontations occur in a low-light or no-light environment, which is why tactical shooters must shoot with speed and accuracy when the sights are not visible, and the target is barely visible. A tactical shooter should be able to shoot with one hand while holding the flashlight in the other hand, but having a gun-mounted light and using flash-and-shoot is usually more effective. If you have a reliable partner behind cover, you let your partner flash the aggressor just long enough for you to shoot. You can also point your flashlight at a deadly funnel (chokepoint) and ambush aggressors when they enter the choke point. When using an ambush, try to get behind cover or have some way to conceal your position. After your first shot, your muzzle blast will reveal your position. If your position is revealed and you are not behind reliable cover, shoot and move might be your best option. Another option would be to fire additional shots. Even if you don't hit the aggressor, the additional shots might serve as suppression fire. Using suppression fire is not the same as *spray and pray*, which often happens when police officers panic and fire multiple shots in the direction of a deadly threat.

If you are tracking an active shooter using a flashlight, shot placement might be a problem if your adversary's body is not visible and you don't want to use your flashlight because there might be more than one active shooter. If your adversary is right-handed, your adversary's body is usually to the left of the flashlight. If you fire two quick shots to the left of the flashlight, one at the same level as the flashlight and one about six inches below the flashlight, you might hit the adversary and cause at least some incapacitation. If you use your flashlight to scan for adversaries, it should be a *flash-and-glace* from behind cover, and you should not expose more of your body than necessary. Using flash-and-glance in a low-light or no-light hostile environment can save your life.

If you can use your adversary's flashlight to approximate your adversary's position, your adversary can use a similar technique to approximate your position. When doing a building search or tracking an adversary with a flashlight, briefly flash your flashlight to check the area from behind cover, or briefly flash your flashlight and change your direction of travel, crouch down, or drop into a prone position. You do not want to be where your adversary thinks you might be.

If you use a gun-mounted light or hold your flashlight in one hand and your gun in the other hand, your body will usually be behind your light. If you are holding a gun with your right hand and activating your gun-mounted light with your left thumb, separating your hands will deactivate your light. If you have a gun-mounted light, you will need to use a two-hand grip when using flash-and-shoot or flash-and-glance. If you have a gun-mounted light, having a flashlight will let your shoot with one hand and flash the area with your other hand.

Hollywood Productions

The police dramas on television might be somewhat realistic if a director uses competent technical advisors. What's not realistic is when a bullet hits someone in the chest, and the person immediately dies. On television or in movies, death is determined by the script, not by shot placement or tactical anatomy. Some police officers who watch these movies believe that one-shot kills are common.

If you watch a show where the good guys are standing out in the open with handguns and the bad guys are shooting at the good guys from behind cover with rifles or shotguns and losing, you are looking at a situation that is not likely to happen in the real world. People standing in the open with handguns will have difficulty defeating people shooting at them from behind cover with rifles or shotguns.

A handgun might be better than a rifle or shotgun when doing a building search if the length of the barrel makes weapon retention difficult, but in most cases, you should leave your handgun holstered if you have access to a rifle or shotgun. Comparing a handgun to a high-velocity assault rifle or a shotgun is a lot like trying to decide who stands a better chance of survival after a motorcycle accident: the person driving a truck or the person driving the motorcycle.

Police dramas are one of the few places where you can see a police officer look in one direction, shoot in a different direction, and knock the bad guy halfway across the room with one shot from a handgun. In real life, shooting at a target you can't see is dangerous, and handgun bullets do not have knock-down power.

In defense of police dramas, some of them are more technically correct than the videos taken by cameras mounted on police vehicles. Police reality shows often show police officers making mistakes a trained police officer would not make, such as not watching a suspect's hands, holding a flashlight in the hand you shoot with, or turning your back on a potentially dangerous suspect. Movie producers are wrong about practically every handgun shot being a one-shot kill, but showing an ice pick kill someone instantly is realistic.

In the Old West, face-to-face gunfights rarely occurred. Most Old West gunfights were not fair, and rifles or shotguns were often used against people armed with a handgun. Old West movies are more accurate when they show bushwhackers ambushing people or back shooters shooting people in the back than when they show someone in a white hat hunting down and killing a gang of outlaws.

Today's concept of fairness is similar to the Old West concept of fairness. Using overwhelming force to defeat dangerous criminals is still acceptable. In the Old West, they used posses, and in today's world, we use SWAT teams. If you need help controlling a deadly threat, call for backup. Years ago, not waiting for backup was called *tombstone courage*. If a situation is dire and you don't have time to wait for backup, you will need to depend on your shooting skills and tactical skills.

Fix the Problem, Not the Blame

One thing Old-West gunfighters and trick shooters had in common was their willingness to practice their shooting skills. Unlike most police officers, it is doubtful that most professional gunfighters or trick shooters would consider shooting 50 rounds per year acceptable practice. Most professional gunfighters believed regular and realistic practice improved their performance in the real world, and they practiced with their guns the way a card sharp practices with cards.

If there is one thing tactical shooters should try to learn from competitive target shooters, it's the value of dedication, hard work, and practice. Competitive target shooters practice almost every week, shoot thousands of rounds per year, and spend years developing their skills. Most police officers do not shoot more than 50 rounds per year if they are not required to qualify more than once a year. Rather than use targets based on tactical anatomy, most police departments use the same targets that target shooters use.

It's hard to understand why competitive target shooters work as hard as they do to win matches and most police officers do not work nearly as hard learning tactical handgun skills that could save their lives. Maybe it's because most police officers believe getting killed in the line of duty is something that happens to someone else but not to them.

Regarding firearms training, some departments are more concerned about cost-effectiveness than combat effectiveness and worry more about being politically correct than teaching officers the correct way to shoot. Police officers spend more time writing reports than getting into gunfights, but the mistakes you make when writing a report do not get you or your partner killed and do not generate multimillion-dollar lawsuits because you killed an innocent person.

When trying to be combat-effective, your goal is to cause immediate or timely incapacitation, and the three elements you need are speed, accuracy, and good aim points. *Speed* is measured by how long it takes to shoot, *accuracy* is measured by whether you hit what you are aiming at, and *aim points* are measured by how quickly a bullet that hits the aim point causes incapacitation.

Most police officers do not get killed in a gunfight because they are too slow. Most police officers get killed because their shooting skills and tactical skills were not good enough to keep them alive. It's hard to say police officers have good shooting skills when they miss the people they are shooting at 30 percent of the time, and it's hard to say they have good tactical skills when they fail to use available cover, use an isosceles shooting stance, or aim at the center of mass.

Instead of fixing the blame, fix the problem. Federal agencies, such as the FBI and DEA, constantly improve their firearms training. Most police officers would not qualify if they had to meet FBI or DEA qualification standards.

HOW TO STOP A KNIFE ATTACK

In today's world, knife fights are extremely uncommon, and people with advanced knife-fighting skills are even less common. A knife expert armed with an ice pick and be far more dangerous than an amateur armed with a ka-bar fighting knife. Most police officers are not killed by people who have been trained to use a knife, and most of the weapons used to cut or stab police officers are not high-quality fighting knives. In most cases, the people who kill police officers with a knife have no more skill with a knife than the average person, and the weapon they use to cut or stab a police officer might be a kitchen knife, a cheap folding knife, a box cutter, a Phillips screwdriver, or a sharp piece of metal or glass.

Even if they realize someone armed with a knife might be getting ready to attack, most police officers do not have the tactical or shooting skills you would need to stop the attack. The two most important tactical skills are moving away from the knife or moving the knife away from your body. The most essential shooting skill is shot placement. You need to hit a body part that causes immediate incapacitation, such as a shot that immediately causes a loss of mobility, unconsciousness, or death. A center-of-mass body shot seldom causes immediate incapacitation, but a center-of-mass headshot almost always causes immediate incapacitation.

A shot that hits the midline of the upper chest might sever the spinal cord and cause an immediate loss of mobility, but a shot to the upper chest that stops the heart might not cause incapacitation or 10 or 15 seconds, which might be enough time to complete a knife attack. If you are using a body shot to stop a knife attack, try to make the shot while you are moving away from the knife. A police officer who has not been trained to shoot a moving target or move and shoot at the same time is unlikely to fire any shots that cause immediate incapacitation.

Verbal commands, such as "drop your knife," might be effective if the person threatening to kill you is stationary, but they are seldom effective if the person threatening you with a knife is moving toward you. If someone is running at you with a knife and you have time to say anything, yelling "Drop the knife or I'll shoot!" might help you justify the use of deadly force. Since this book is about handgun techniques, discussing tasers or chemical sprays is beyond the scope of this book, but it appears the use of non-lethal weapons is becoming more common.

After a knife attack starts, you need to plan your defense immediately. Good training can save your life, and poor training can get you killed. FBI and DEA agents are more likely to have the skills they need to defend against a knife attack than police officers. Most people who teach police officers how to defend against a knife attack have never done a knife disarm or been in a knife fight and have never used a handgun to stop a knife attack, which is why most of what they teach is useless.

The following methods for stopping a knife attack are based on personal experience and tactical anatomy. Since the authors are not lawyers or police administrators, it's the reader's responsibility to determine if these techniques are legal or if they violate departmental administrative orders.

A person threatening to kill you with a knife can be stationary or moving. A stationary person standing 30 feet away is usually less of a threat than a stationary person standing 10 feet away. A person attacking you with a knife and running at you from 10 feet is usually more of a threat than someone running at you with a knife from 30 feet. If a person attacks you with a knife from 10 feet away, your best option might be to move the knife away from your body or move your body away from the knife before you try to use your handgun.

At what point you have a legal right to use deadly force to stop a knife attack depends on the circumstances. You will probably need to explain why you used deadly force to end a deadly threat instead of using non-lethal force. You might also need to explain why you considered someone threatening you with a knife a deadly threat. Was it reasonable to believe the person could easily carry out the threat?

Many people fail to realize that how a police officer handles a deadly threat depends on judgment and skill. To a large extent, the amount and kind of training a police officer has will determine how much force needs to be used to stop a knife attack and not get injured. A well-trained police officer might be able to resolve a deadly knife threat without using deadly force and without getting hurt, whereas a poorly trained police officer might use deadly force and still get killed. More and better training might be a good starting point if police departments want to reduce the number of people shot and killed by police because of knife attacks.

Police officers who do not understand how people attack with a knife will have difficulty protecting themselves from a knife attack. If you are trying to teach police officers how to protect themselves against a knife attack, demonstrate the type of knife attacks they are most likely to encounter and show them how to defend themselves against the same kind of knife attacks. When teaching a police officer how to attack with a knife, you can use a soft rubber knife for the attack and give the officer being attacked protective gear, such as gloves and eye protection.

After the officers understand the nature of knife attacks, teach them how to defend against similar knife attacks. Choreographing the attacks and defenses to help officers learn the movements can be useful, but at some point, you need to randomize the attacks and not tell the officers in advance what kind of knife attack you will use next. Not knowing what the next knife attack will be will stop the officers from starting a knife defense before you start the attack.

After the officers understand knife attacks, show them how to defend against a knife attack with a handgun. Using a handgun should include using a two-hand grip and a one-hand grip and using the empty hand for offense or defense.

For police officers to stand a good chance of stopping a knife attack when the attacker is running at them, they must be able to hit a moving target and shoot and move at the same time. It's easy to understand why police officers who have never learned these skills might believe that if someone is threatening your life with a knife, waiting for the person to run at you with the knife will increase your risk of getting killed. On the other hand, shooting a stationary person who threatens to kill you will a knife increases your risk of being arrested or sued.

Most police officers do not have the shooting skills they need to stop a knife attack when the attacker is running at them. Not only do most police officers lack advanced shooting skills, such as shooting a moving target or moving and shooting at the same time, but according to some studies, police officers currently have a 50% hit rate. A 50% hit rate means they miss the people they are shooting at about 50% of the time. You have no chance of stopping a knife attack with a handgun if you miss, and even if you don't miss, you are unlikely to cause immediate incapacitation and stop and knife attack if none of your bullets hit the brain stem or spinal cord. You can miss your target multiple times and still qualify, but one miss can get you killed when you try to stop a knife attack with a handgun.

Contrary to what many police officers believe, the 21-foot rule is not a law, and it does not automatically give you the right to shoot someone who is threatening to kill you with a knife and less than 21 feet away. Before you use deadly force, you need to consider other factors, such as whether the person threatening you with a knife can carry out the threat or is there a risk of wounding innocent civilians if you use deadly force? Negotiation or non-lethal devices might be a better option than deadly force, but deadly force should be available as an option if negotiation or non-lethal techniques fail. It's dangerous to use a non-lethal device against a knife attack if you don't have another officer standing by who can intervene and use deadly force if a non-lethal device fails.

The 21-foot rule is partially based on the premise that a police officer cannot draw a gun and stop a knife attack if the attacker starts the attack from less than 21 feet away. The problem with this premise is that it makes several assumptions that are not realistic.

1. Police officers who anticipate a deadly threat should have their guns out of the holster and their fingers off the trigger until they determine if the threat is real. If the threat is confirmed, you should immediately point your gun at the person responsible for the deadly threat. You can use a two-hand grip and raise the gun to shoulder level if you have enough time, or point and shoot as quickly as you can with one hand. At close range, it's easier to point and shoot with one hand than with two hands, and you can use the empty hand for offense or defense.

2. Another unrealistic assumption is that a police officer will not move away from the attacker when the attacker moves toward the police officer. Moving in a lateral direction is usually safer than moving backward, and a well-trained police officer can move and shoot at the same time.
3. How far you should be from someone threatening to kill you with a knife depends on the situation. Being closer than 21 feet might be reasonable if you can position yourself behind a barrier that makes it difficult for the person with the knife to attack you, or you might move farther away if you are waiting for backup.

The 21-rule also fails to consider the possibility that tactical and shooting skills are more important than the distance between a police officer and the person with the knife. Regardless of the distance between the officer and a person who is threatening to kill you will a knife, a well-trained officer is more likely to survive than a poorly trained officer. Why would anyone believe police officers who miss the people they are shooting at about 70% stand a good chance of stopping any knife attack with a handgun? Bad training produces bad results.

Being aware of what's happening around you is one of the best ways to stop a surprise knife attack. If you see what might be preparation for a knife attack, try to move away from the person who you believe might attack you, watch the person's hands, and be prepared to take offensive or defensive action if the person tries to get closer. If you are taken by surprise, action will usually be faster than reaction, and you might not be able to stop a knife attack. Recognizing a possible knife attack before it becomes an actual knife attack can save your life.

The belief that police officers learn most of what they know about stopping a knife attack from watching television or movies might be true, and what they learn from television or movies might be more useful than what they learned in a police academy. Hollywood stunts such as shooting or kicking a knife out of someone's hand or shooting someone in the foot to stop a knife attack are not realistic, but techniques such as throwing dirt in someone's face or using a shovel to defend yourself against might work. Using a broom to push someone back who is attacking you with a knife might give you enough time to draw your gun.

After you stop a knife attack, do not relax too soon. Never assume an attack is over just because the attacker dropped a knife. Since your attacker might have more than one knife or have a different kind of weapon, stay on high alert until the attacker is subdued and searched. Check the area for other potential dangers, and do not forget to render immediate first aid if the attacker is injured. Have someone check your body for knife wounds you might not be aware of. If someone stabs you in the chest, do not assume the wound is minor because you don't see much blood. Immediately seek medical help because you might have internal bleeding.

Any knife attack is potentially deadly, but how someone holds a knife may indicate their skill level. People who hold a knife over the top of their head before they attack are less likely to be trained than people who use a tactical stance (boxer's stance) and hold the tip of the knife at or near shoulder level. Having the empty hand in front of the knife will make it easier to protect the knife and the hand that controls it, but people with knife training might move the knife hand in front of the empty hand if they see an opening and decide to attack.

If someone attacks you with a knife, do not focus all your attention on the knife. Be aware that your adversary's empty hand and other body parts, such as the feet, can be used for offense or defense. If you see an opening, you can use your empty hand for offense or defense, or you can use it to restrict the movement of your adversary's knife so you can use your gun.

Never assume that a knife that doesn't look dangerous is not dangerous. A knife is any weapon capable of inflicting a cut or stab wound. Even though a large knife, such as a ka-bar, is potentially more dangerous than a small folding knife because it can inflict deeper stab wounds than a small pocket knife, both can cut major arteries and cause serious injuries or death. An ice pick seldom produces deep cuts, but it can kill someone by penetrating the brainstem, and it might be able to reach the heart after it penetrates a bullet-resistant vest.

Years ago, when most police officers carried a knife, one of the authors carried Colt 45 Combat Commander and a sheath knife whenever executing circuit court orders that allowed you to use whatever force is reasonable and necessary to enter.

An occupant tried to cut me after executing one of these orders, and using a handgun might have caused civilian casualties. After an empty-hand disarm failed, I got cut, and the knife disarm turned into a knife fight. (This was not my first empty-hand knife disarm, but it was the first time I got cut. I was never injured when doing empty-hand gun disarms.). Because of using my knife instead of my gun to incapacitate the person who cut me, I didn't have civilian causalities. The cut was minor, and it didn't require medical attention.

Using a block or parry to move a knife away from your body or grabbing and holding the knife in place is not a knife disarm, but it might give you enough time to draw your handgun. Using these techniques is usually safer than using an empty-hand disarm, and they might give you time to draw and use your handgun.

Most of the choreographed knife disarming techniques that police officers learn are useless when used against someone trying to kill you. The only time police officers should try to do an empty-hand knife disarm or use a knife as a weapon is when they have no other option. Using your knife as a weapon might be your best option if someone tries to grab your gun. Check with your department before you carry a knife on duty. Because of liability, some departments let their officers carry a rescue knife but not a tactical knife.

If you work for a department that lets you carry any knife that is easy to conceal and carry, a sheath knife is more reliable and stronger than a folding knife. If you wear a bullet-resistant vest covered by a shirt, your knife will not be visible if you attach it to your vest. If the knife is in a sheath and you attach the sheath to the front panel of your vest, you can quickly draw the knife with either hand. The knife will be easier to draw if the handle hangs down from the sheath. If you might use the knife for self-defense, study the relationship between knife wounds and tactical anatomy so you know what to expect if you use a knife for self-defense.

If you are working at night or in a dark room, you might be able to blind someone who attacks you with a knife by flashing a bright light into both eyes. After you flash the light into the eyes, moving quickly to a new location will make it harder for the person holding the knife to find you. If you have a gun-mounted light, the flash-and-shoot technique can be very effective against a knife attack: flash the eyes with your gun-mounted light, shoot, and then move or flash the light into the eyes and then move and shoot at the same time. When using a flash and move technique, keep both eyes open and use a target focus instead of a front-sight focus because finding your front sight when you have almost no light is almost impossible.

Knife attacks are dangerous even for people with good shooting and good tactical skills, and luck will sometimes determine the outcome more than skill. If escape is not an option, you need to be decisive and react without hesitation. Some people may back down if they believe you might use deadly force, and other people would rather risk getting killed than be arrested. There is no perfect way to stop a knife attack with a handgun, but good training will reduce of risk of getting killed.

During a conflict in the Philippines that started around the late 1800s, the U.S. Military discovered that the Islamic Moro natives who lived in the southern Philippines were extremely fierce warriors and very good at waging suicide attacks when armed with nothing but a short, wavy sword called a *kris*. Contrary to popular belief, it was not the .45 caliber Colt revolver but the 12-gauge Winchester Model 1897 shotgun that proved to be the best weapon for stopping a charging Moro native. Contrary to popular belief, Model 1911 .45 ACP pistols were not used during this conflict. If you happen to have one available, a shotgun is more likely to cause immediate incapacitation and stop a knife attack than a handgun. At a distance between 5 and 15 feet, it might take slightly less time to aim a shotgun than to aim a handgun because the pellets will have started to spread, and just one 00 buckshot pellet might cause almost as much tissue damage as one .45 caliber bullet.

Having a .45 caliber handgun might make you feel more secure, and having a large opening at the end of your barrel might make the people you aim your pistol at feel less secure, but a 9mm pistol and a .45 caliber pistol will be equally effective if your shot placement is good. If you want to under the difference between good and bad shot placement, you need to study tactical anatomy.

Tactical Knives

The first Ka-Bar is similar to the knife the Marine Raiders used during World War II, and the second one is a modern version of the Ka-Bar. The Ka-Bar is considered a fighting-utility knife. The Fairbairn-Sykes (F-S) Fighting Knife was used by British Commandos during World War II and is similar to the fighting knives (stilettos) that the U. S. Marine Raiders and Black Devils used. The Ka-Bar has a stronger blade than a stiletto and has probably killed more soldiers than any other tactical knife. Most traditional tactical knives had a fixed blade, crossguard, and a pommel that could be used as an impact weapon.

TACTICAL-KNIFE ANATOMY

Traditional and Modern Ka-Bars: Single-Edged Tactical Knives

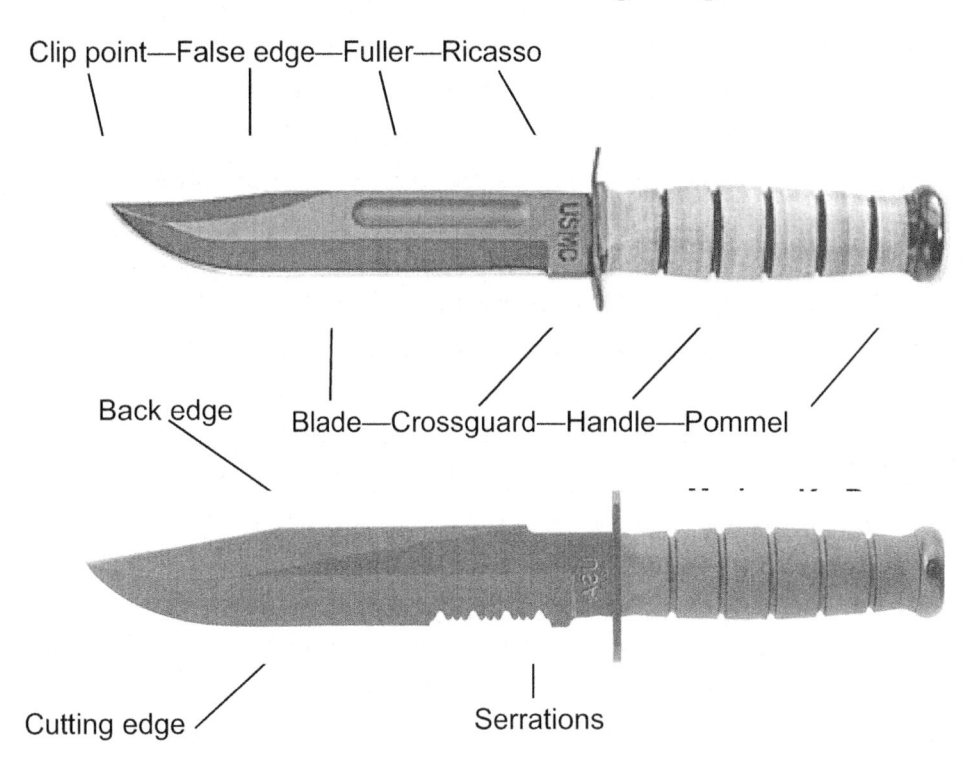

Clip point—False edge—Fuller—Ricasso

Back edge

Blade—Crossguard—Handle—Pommel

Cutting edge

Serrations

Fairbairn-Sykes Fighting Knife: Double-Edged Stiletto

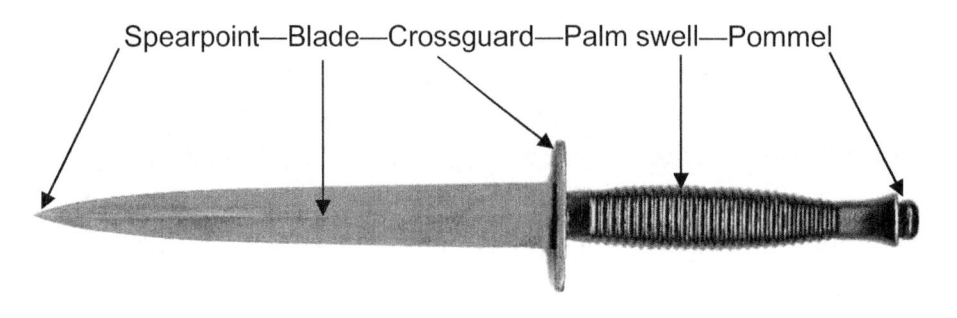

Spearpoint—Blade—Crossguard—Palm swell—Pommel

Anatomy of a Knife Attack

You cannot defend yourself against a knife attack until you understand the nature of a knife attack. Most knife attacks are carried out by cutting or stabbing a victim or hitting the victim with the pommel of a knife, which is a knob on the end of a knife's handle. Pommel strikes are rare, but they can inflict serious injuries.

When a police officer defends against a knife attack, the first line of defense is usually a handgun or a shotgun. If you have no other weapons, you can use a knife to defend yourself against a knife. Defending against a knife attack with a knife is usually safer than using empty hand techniques, such as blocks, parries, or grabs. The most effective empty-hand techniques are evasion, moving away from a knife, and eye strikes. Moving a knife away from your body and shooting at the same time is also a good technique. Most of the knife disarming techniques police officers learn in a police academy are useless against someone with even basic knife skills.

Some knife attacks start with a grab or a push. Failure to move away quickly when someone grabs or pushes you can get cut or stabbed. Another common knife technique is to pass close to the right side of your victim and then stab your victim in the back with your right hand and keep walking.

If a stab wound to the back severs the thoracic spinal cord, paralysis will be immediate. If a stab wound to the back of the neck severs the upper cervical cord, incapacitation will be immediate. If a knife passes through the opening at the base of the skull (foreman magnum) and disrupts the brainstem, incapacitation will be immediate. If your adversary attacks the front or side of your body before walking past you, a blade that enters under the chin (submandibular triangle) or into the ear canal and disrupts the brainstem will cause immediate incapacitation.

Maintaining a six-foot separation from people close to you will help you avoid a knife attack. If you can see the attack coming, you might have time to move away from the knife or move the knife away from your body. If you can increase the distance between you and your attacker, you might have time to fire a shot. If you are fast enough, the ideal position is behind your attacker.

Besides a knife wound that severs the upper cervical spinal cord or disrupts the brainstem, knife wounds seldom cause immediate incapacitation. If a knife wound stops your heart and you have a handgun in your hand, you will have about 10 to 15 seconds to shoot your adversary. You might be able to kill the person who killed you in less than ten seconds. If a knife severs your carotid artery, you will usually be functional for more than 15 seconds. If you are defending against a knife attack with a handgun, a skilled knife fighter will attempt to disable the hand or arm holding your gun rather than stab you in the heart or cut a carotid artery.

Someone who attacks you with a knife is a deadly threat. A knife is any handheld instrument capable of causing a stab (puncture) wound or a cut (incised) wound. A stab wound results from pushing a pointed object into human tissue, and a cut wound results from pushing or pulling a sharp object across human tissue. A screwdriver can inflict a deep stab wound, and a large glass fragment can sever large blood vessels. Knife attacks may cause paralysis or death, and many people fear getting cut or stabbed more than they fear getting.

PRIMARY KNIFE TARGETS

Most primary targets are located along the midline—trachea (windpipe), upper cervical spinal cord, foramen magnum, the soft spot under the chin, heart, aorta, or pulmonary artery—or close to the midline—eyes, carotid arteries, subclavian arteries, or kidneys. The ear canals are not located close to the midline, but they are openings that can give you access to the brainstem, which is located along the midline. The knife hand and the arm that controls the knife hand (knife arm) are primary targets, and the empty hand and the arm that controls the empty hand are secondary targets. The top of the head is not a target for most tactical knives, but it might be a target for a knife—such as a Gung Ho knife or a Gurkha Kukri Knife—large enough to split the skull (cranium) in half.

It's unlikely you would stab someone in the back, sever the thoracic spinal cord, and then penetrate the heart or stab someone in the throat and sever the upper cervical spinal cord.

Midline

Eyes

Trachea

Heart

Abdomen

Groin

Aortic Arch

Anterior Heart

Pulmonary Artery

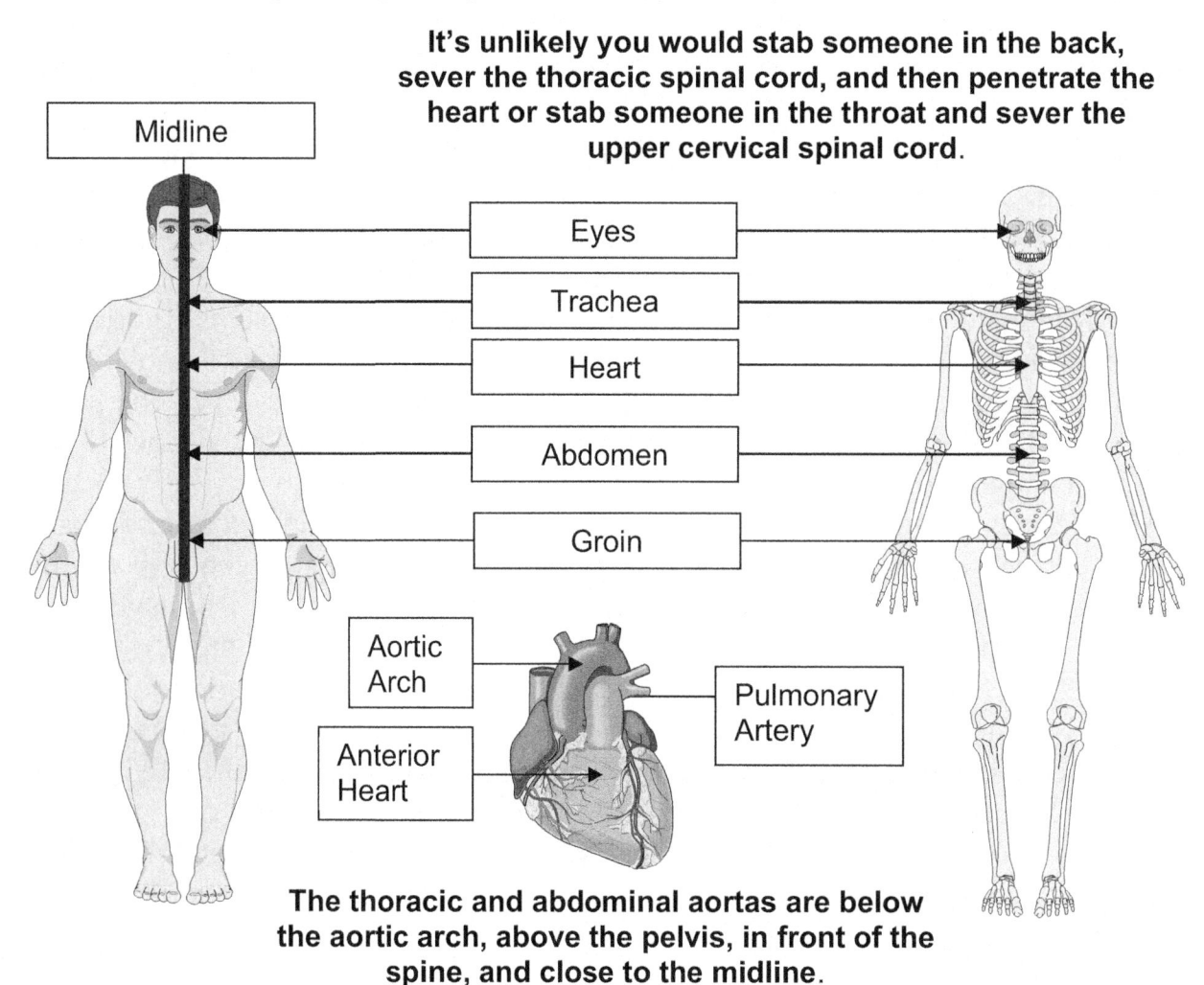

The thoracic and abdominal aortas are below the aortic arch, above the pelvis, in front of the spine, and close to the midline.

87

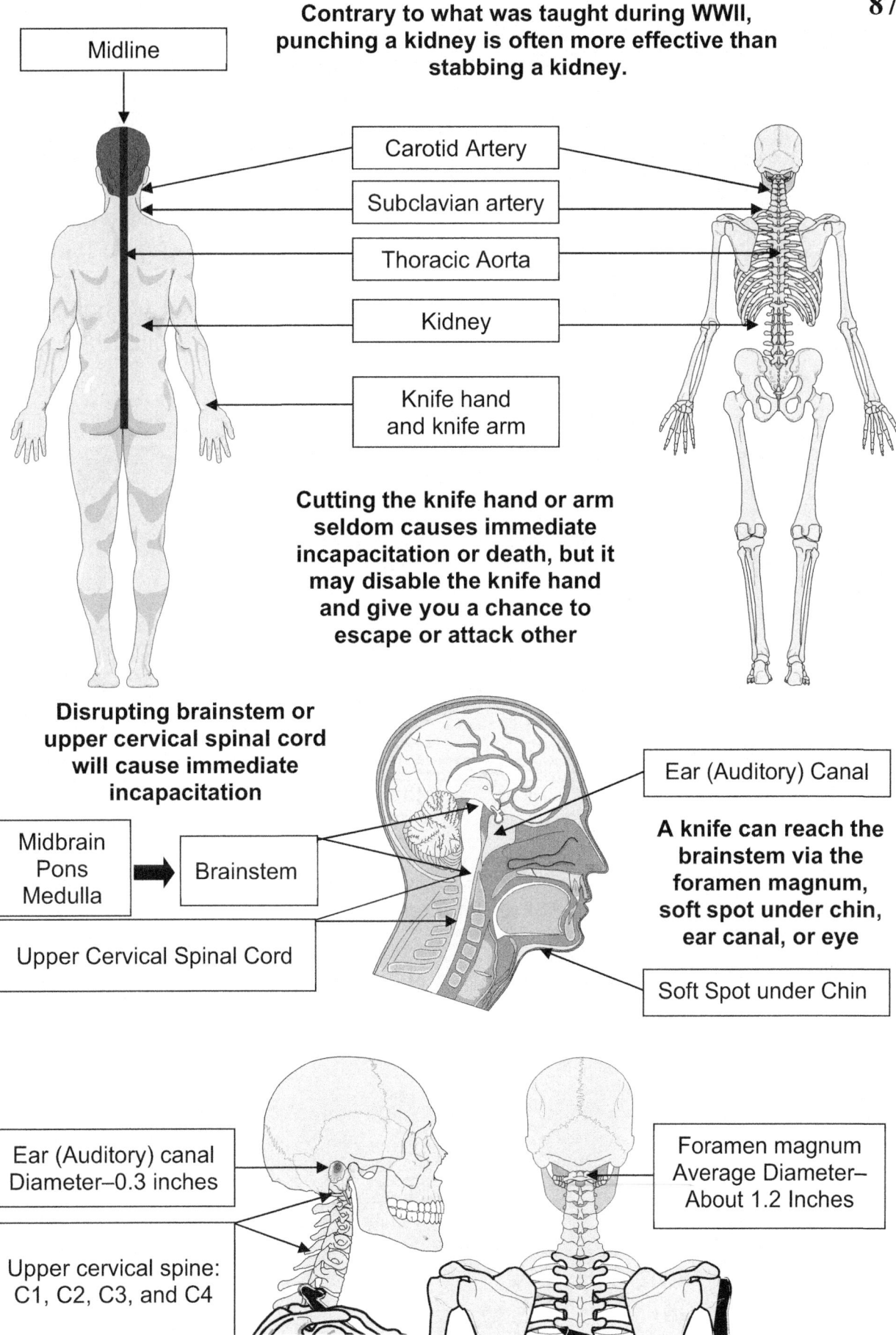

Contrary to what was taught during WWII, punching a kidney is often more effective than stabbing a kidney.

- Midline
- Carotid Artery
- Subclavian artery
- Thoracic Aorta
- Kidney
- Knife hand and knife arm

Cutting the knife hand or arm seldom causes immediate incapacitation or death, but it may disable the knife hand and give you a chance to escape or attack other

Disrupting brainstem or upper cervical spinal cord will cause immediate incapacitation

- Midbrain, Pons, Medulla → Brainstem
- Upper Cervical Spinal Cord
- Ear (Auditory) Canal
- Soft Spot under Chin

A knife can reach the brainstem via the foramen magnum, soft spot under chin, ear canal, or eye

- Ear (Auditory) canal Diameter – 0.3 inches
- Upper cervical spine: C1, C2, C3, and C4
- Foramen magnum Average Diameter – About 1.2 Inches

SECONDARY KNIFE TARGETS

Attacking secondary targets may cause significant damage, but these targets are unlikely to cause rapid incapacitation, and they are often hard to reach during a typical confrontation. Severing the spinal cord below C4 is more likely to cause immobility than incapacitation. The femoral artery is hard to reach, but severing it may cause delayed incapacitation or death. The temporal bone is easy to find but stabbing it seldom causes incapacitation or death. Because of osseous tissue (bone), the soft spot below the ear will not give you easy access to the brainstem. Stabbing the axilla (armpit) may cause rapid incapacitation if the blade penetrates the heart, thoracic aorta, or pulmonary artery.

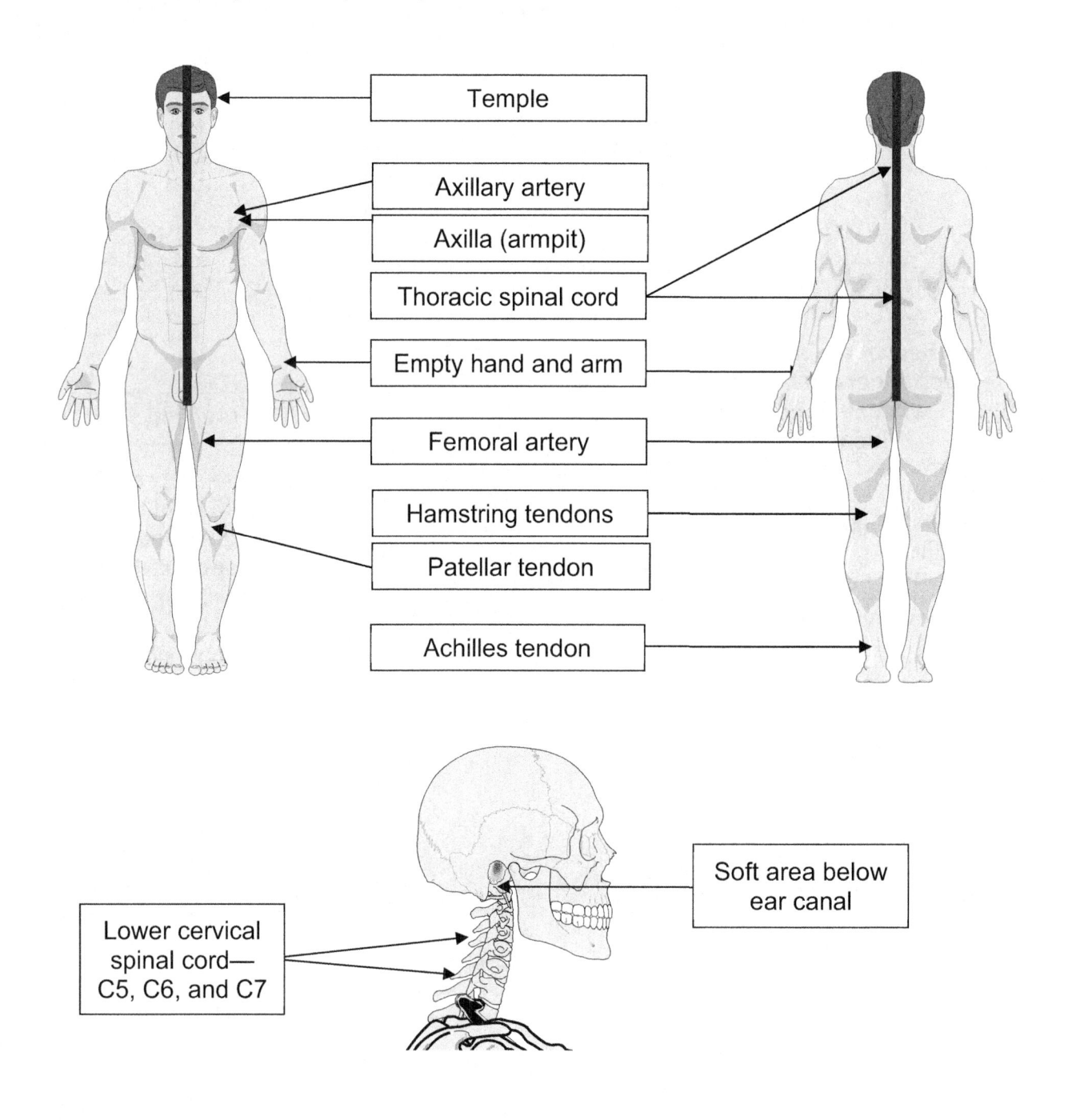

- Temple
- Axillary artery
- Axilla (armpit)
- Thoracic spinal cord
- Empty hand and arm
- Femoral artery
- Hamstring tendons
- Patellar tendon
- Achilles tendon

- Lower cervical spinal cord—C5, C6, and C7
- Soft area below ear canal

If You Anticipate a Knife Attack

- Maintain as much distance as possible from your adversary.
- Push your attacker away from you with a tool, such as a shovel.
- Keep track of your adversary's hands and what they are doing.
- Take a defensive stance and aim your handgun or shotgun.
- Without being submissive, try to negotiate a peaceful solution.
- Call for backup or ask bystanders to call the police.
- If you are attacked: defend and counterattack without hesitation.
- Use barriers, furniture, walls, or stairs to improve your position.
- Look for things you can use as a shield, such as clothing or chairs.
- Pick up things you can throw, such as rocks, sand, dirt, or fluids.
- Look for supplemental weapons, such as a potent chemical spray.
- Do not try an empty-hand knife disarm if you have other options.
- Do not stand your ground if you can safely retreat.

Fight the Person, Not the Knife

Rather than focus on the knife, focus on your adversary. If you focus on the knife, you might not be able to defend yourself if an adversary attacks you with an empty-hand technique, such as a punch, stranglehold, or eye strike. Furthermore, disarming adversaries will not stop them from attacking you with empty-hand techniques or regaining control of their knives unless you restrain them.

No Real Winners

Knife fights are rare because your chances of winning a knife fight without getting cut or stabbed are very small unless one person has much better knife skills or more luck than the other. A person who walks away from a knife fight is usually declared the winner, but more than a few winners have died a few days later because of injuries inflicted during a knife fight.

Check Your Body

If you get involved in a knife conflict, immediately have someone check your body for wounds after the fight is over. Puncture wounds to the heart might not be painful, and blood loss might not be apparent. Untreated infection because of a knife wound can be fatal. A small pocket knife concealed by someone's armpit might seem insignificant, but it might also be a valid reason for using deadly force.

Stopping a Knife Attack with a Shotgun

After decades of experience, the U.S. military has proved that a shotgun is more effective against a knife attack than a .45 caliber handgun. Despite this proof, some people still believe that one body shot from a 1911 series handgun will instantly stop a knife attack. If you try to stop a knife attack with a body shot from a .45 caliber bullet, you might not live long enough to regret your mistake. At best, looking at the large hole at the end of a .45 caliber barrel might convince someone that dropping their knife might be a good idea.

From a police perspective, you will probably not have a shotgun in your hand when you need one. While police officers are on duty, they usually carry a handgun unless they enter jail with a prisoner or testify at a trial. If they have access to a shotgun, it will probably be in the trunk of a car or locked in a shotgun rack. The only time you might have a shotgun in your hand when facing a knife attack is when a dispatcher tells you a subject might be armed with a knife.

Having a shotgun available today is less common than before most police officers carried a tactical rifle. A high-velocity tactical rifle is also effective against a knife attack, but overpenetration or misses might result in civilian casualties.

At close range (0-21 feet), a 12-gauge shotgun loaded with buckshot and having an 18-inch barrel can be very effective against multiple adversaries who are facing you or using a flanking maneuver to circumvent your cover. A shotgun will usually cause more tissue damage than a handgun at close range. The diameter of a near-contact wound will usually be larger than 0.729 inches, which is the bore diameter of a 12-gauge shotgun and more than twice the diameter of a .357 Magnum. The distance 00 buckshot starts to spread beyond a 4-inch circle is usually 5-10 feet.

During World War I, U.S. soldiers fighting in trenches discovered the value of having both a handgun and shotgun (trench gun) available when facing enemy soldiers in dark, narrow trenches at close range. Most trench guns had a small bead at the end of the barrel, but a bead would have been hard to see in a dark trench.

During the Philippine conflict, the military used 12-gauge shotguns because it was easier to stop someone at close range with nine tightly-packed 00 buckshot pellets than with a .45-caliber bullet. At a distance between 5 and 15 feet, it's easier to fire a combat-effective shot with a shotgun than with a handgun, and one 00 buckshot pellet might cause almost as much tissue damage as one .45 caliber bullet.

The maximum combat-effective range for 00 buckshot is about 75 feet, and even if you aim correctly, half of the pellets will usually miss if you are trying to make a headshot. The most reliable combat-effective distance for 00 buckshot is about 20 feet, and a competent tactical shooter should be able to use a target focus and put some of the pellets in a 5-inch circle at this distance.

A shotgun that groups most of the pellets near the center of a pattern tends to be more combat effective than one that hollows out the center and increases the density of pellets near the edge. Before using a shotgun, check the pattern.

At 0 to 21 feet, buckshot does not drop enough to make trajectory a concern, and most of your adversaries will not be moving fast enough to make leading your targets necessary. Even at close range, it's possible to miss if you don't aim the shotgun. At close range, follow the same advice given to pheasant hunters: keep your eye on the bird and not the barrel or the bead, which means use a target focus.

Using a front-sight focus might be practical if your target is stationary and you are trying to make a precise shot with shotgun slugs, but use a target focus for most close-quarter combat. When using a shotgun to stop a knife attack, pellets are less likely to cause overpenetration causalities than shotgun slugs.

Without correct and regular practice, you cannot maintain or improve shotgun or handgun shooting skills. The basic skills you need when shooting a shotgun or handgun are similar. To be proficient with a shotgun, you need a good grip, a smooth trigger pull, a good stance, and a hold on the weapon that helps you control recoil.

Since shotguns are not carried in a holster, a common problem is knowing where to put a shotgun if you need both hands to handcuff a suspect. If you are using a handgun, you can reholster your gun. If you don't have a sling on your shotgun, it might not be safe to handcuff a suspect until backup arrives.

Some shotguns are not drop-safe, which means you might have an accidental discharge if you drop the shotgun or hit someone with the butt of the shotgun. If a shotgun is not drop-safe, be extremely careful about where you point the barrel when you have a shotgun shell in the chamber. Do not carry a shotgun until you know if it has a drop safety. Most new shotguns have a drop safety.

If you carry a tactical shotgun, you need to practice loading and unloading the shotgun. Loading a shotgun tends to be easier than unloading a shotgun. Shotgun accidents often occur because someone failed to remove all the rounds from a tube magazine when unloading the shotgun or the next person who used the shotgun failed to verify the shotgun was empty.

After you learn how to shoot a shotgun, you must learn the different carry positions and shotgun retention techniques. When using a shotgun to counter a knife attack, getting close enough for someone to grab your shotgun can be a deadly mistake. If someone grabs your shotgun, the safest response is to point the shotgun at your adversary and pull the trigger. If you cannot get the barrel pointed at your adversary, you need to use a shotgun retention technique. If a shotgun retention technique turns into a wrestling match, keep the shotgun's barrel pointed away from your body with one hand and draw your handgun with the other hand. If your adversary releases the shotgun, grab the shotgun, and move away. If your adversary does not release the shotgun, using your handgun might be your only option.

If using your handgun is not an option and you have access to a knife, the hands, arms, neck, or eyes are usually your best targets. Biting your attacker's arm or striking your attacker's eyes are also options, but these options are usually less effective than using your handgun.

Even if you have a shotgun, standing in the open when facing a knife attack is more dangerous than standing behind a barricade, such as a tree. A right-handed shotgun shooter can shift the shotgun to the left shoulder and use the left eye when shooting around the left side of a barricade. Shifting the shotgun to the opposite shoulder usually works better for most shotgun shooters than switching to a weak-hand grip. When using a handgun, shifting to the weak hand is usually easier.

Most people have a greater fear of being shot by a shotgun than being shot by a handgun, and hearing you load a shotgun might draw attention to the fact you have a shotgun. This belief might be somewhat valid, but waiting until the last minute to load a shotgun can be disastrous if you have a loading malfunction and someone attacks you with a knife while trying to fix a malfunction and load a shotgun. If you have a shotgun malfunction when someone attacks you with a knife, you can use the shotgun's barrel to push your attacker back, which might give you enough time to move away from your attacker and draw your handgun.

The basic tactical positions for a shotgun are high-ready position, low-ready position, retention position, and carry position. The *high-ready position* tends to be the most accurate position because the top of the shotgun is aligned with your line of sight. When using a high-ready position, seat the butt in your shoulder pocket and press your cheek against the stock. If an adversary is not more than 21 feet away and it appears a knife attack might be imminent, use a high-ready position.

The *low-ready position* is similar to the high-ready position, but the top of the shotgun is below your line of sight. This position might be used when you try to de-escalate a potential knife attack and your adversary is more than 21 feet away.

When using the *retention position*, the stock is under your shooting arm, which brings the end of the barrel closer to your body and makes it harder for someone to grab the barrel. The shotgun is angled downward and pointed toward the ground when using a *carry position*. If you are searching for someone armed with a knife, use a retention position instead of a carry position.

To practice using a target focus with an empty shotgun: hold the shotgun in a low-ready position, pick a target, close your eyes, mount the gun by shifting into a high-ready position, and align the barrel with your target while your eyes are still closed. When you believe the shotgun is aligned with your target, open your eyes, and check the alignment. The goal is to have the shotgun aligned with the target every time you open your eyes. You can use the same technique to practice aligning the barrel of a handgun with a target. Pulling the trigger when you believe the barrel of a shotgun or pistol is aligned with a target is not required.

A second way to practice using a target focus at 21 feet is to use a shotgun that has the sights covered or removed. If you consistently get a good pattern at 21 feet with the sights covered or removed, you should be able to use a target focus during a deadly confrontation if the target is no more than 21 feet away. Even if you do most of your practicing with birdshot, you should verify your ability to use a target focus at the same distance when using buckshot.

When stopping a knife attack, a tactical shotgun shooter needs to use a target focus and hit the correct aim points when shooting a person 21 feet away or closer. If you were using a handgun, the best aim points would be a headshot or a heart shot. A headshot would cause immediate incapacitation, and a heart shot would probably cause timely incapacitation. A pelvic shot with a handgun is unlikely to cause incapacitation or immobilization. A pelvic shot with a shotgun is unlikely to cause incapacitation but might cause a loss of mobility that stops a knife attack. Using a pelvic shot would not be safe if the person armed with a knife also had a gun.

If you make a heart shot with 00 buckshot at 45 feet, some of the pellets may miss the heart, but if you are getting good patterns with your shotgun, the number of pellets that penetrate or perforate the heart might be sufficient to cause cardiac arrest. If you try to make a heart shot with 00 buckshot at 75 feet, causing a heart attack is less likely. A few pellets may hit the heart, and others miss the entire body.

If your adversary is standing sideways and you hit the correct aim point for the heart, some of the pellets may hit the body but not penetrate far enough to reach the heart or the large vessels above the heart. It's also possible for a pellet to penetrate the heart and have no visible effect until hemorrhage causes death.

If you make a headshot with 00 buckshot at 21 feet or less, the probability is very high that you will cause immediate incapacitation. If the distance is 45 feet, your chances of causing immediate incapacitation will decrease. If the distance is 75 feet, none of the pellets may penetrate the skull unless they enter through an eye socket, and your chances of severing the upper cervical spinal cord are not good. At 75 feet, a 9mm bullet might be more effective than 00 buckshot.

Although some police officers believe that a blast from a shotgun will always have one-shot stopping power, you might miss, your adversary might be too far away, or body armor might decrease penetration. If an adversary moves in a lateral direction, shooting with both eyes open will make it easy to track your adversary.

To reduce the recoil you feel when you shoot a shotgun: (1) use a recoil pad and let the force from the recoil spread over most of the surface, (2) keep the butt pressed against your shoulder and do not let it touch your upper arm, and (3) relax your body, lean slightly forward, and roll with the recoil the same way a boxer rolls with a punch. You can also use a stock that's designed to reduce recoil.

Tactical Shotgun Techniques

| High Ready | Low Ready Position | Retention Position |

| Carry Position | High Loading | Retention Loading |

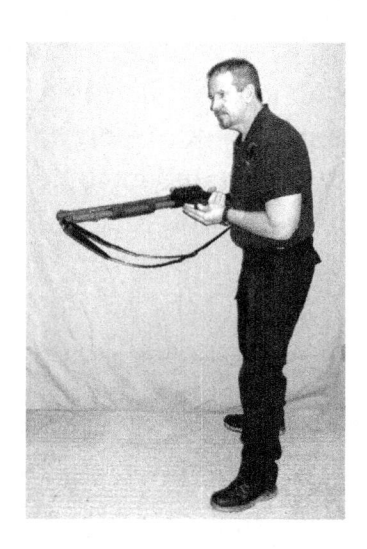

Field of View: You cannot focus on your shotgun and look for adversaries at the same time. Except for when you load with one hand because your other hand is disabled and you need to glance at your shotgun, you should not look at the loading port or the ejecting port when loading a shotgun. You should keep your eyes moving and scan for potential threats.

| Ejection Port Loading | One-Hand Loading | One-Hand Shooting |

| Left Barricade | Retention—Shotgun | Retention—Handgun |

Left Barricade: If you are using a right-handed grip on the stock and need to shoot from the left side of a barricade, switching to a left-handed grip is usually a better option than shifting the stock to your left shoulder (shoulder bump).

Shotgun Retention: If someone grabs the barrel of your shotgun, you can try to aim the shotgun at your adversary and shoot, or you can transition to your handgun and shoot. The aim points for a shotgun are a headshot, heart shot, and pelvic shot. The combat-effective range for a shotgun loaded with 00 buckshot is about 75 feet.

A TACTICAL TARGET FOR HANDGUNS

This target is for tactical shooters instead of target shooters because the only way to get full credit for a shot is to hit the 5-inch circle that represents a headshot or the 5-inch circle that represents a heart shot. A headshot causes immediate incapacitation, and a heart shot might cause timely incapacitation. A person is usually functional for 10 to 15 seconds if a bullet stops the heart. To cause timely incapacitation, you need to survive until the person you shot in the heart is not a deadly threat. Center-of-mass shots might not cause incapacitation until blood loss causes unconsciousness, which could be minutes or hours after someone is wounded.

You could create this tactical target with a paper silhouette and 5-inch paper plates, but the ideal target would be a steel silhouette with two 5-inch gongs. The best material for the silhouette and gongs would be AR500 steel. If you use a silhouette with one gong in the middle of the upper chest, you will be training yourself to make heart shots, but not headshots. A tactical shooter must be able to make both heart shots and headshots

When facing a knife attack, your best option might be one heart shot and two headshots. The heart shot will not cause immediate incapacitation, but even a near miss when trying to make a head shot might slow your adversary down. If your adversary continues to advance, it will be easier to make a headshot when your adversary is closer and moving at a slower rate of speed. If your adversary starts slowing down after a heart shot, it might be safer to move away from your adversary than try to make a headshot.

Scoring a tactical target:
- Headshot—any bullet that hits the 5-inch aim point—5 points
- Heart shot—any bullet that hits the 5-inch aim point—5 points

Optional 4-points: hits above the bottom of the heart-shot circle but not within either circle: shots that hit the neck might damage major blood vessels or the spinal cord, and shots that hit to the side of the heart might damage major blood vessels. Almost any bullet that hits this area will be a significant distraction and might give you enough time to fire additional shots.

Companies that manufacture steel targets should tell you the safe distances for their products. Steel silhouette targets should be at least 75 feet away when using a handgun. Having steel targets closer may increase your risk of being hit by a ricochet. The International Defensive Pistol Association (IDP) believes you can engage steel targets at 30 feet according to Rule 2.14, and Range365 believes 45 feet is the minimum safe distance when engaging steel targets with a handgun.

United States Department of Justice Quarterly Requalification requirements:

- From the 50-yard line, run 25 yards to the 25-yard line and draw and fire four rounds kneeling and four rounds prone in 20 seconds. (8 rounds)
- From the 15-yard line, draw and fire three rounds in 6 seconds. From a ready position, fire four rounds in 5 seconds. (7 rounds)
- From the 7-yard line, draw and fire five rounds in 5 seconds. From a ready position, fire four rounds, reload, and fire four more rounds in 8 seconds. (17 seconds)
- From the 5-yard line, draw and fire three rounds in 3 seconds. Then from a ready position, fire three rounds in 2 seconds and six rounds in 4 seconds. (12 rounds).
- From the 3-yard line, draw and fire three rounds strong hand and three rounds weak hand in 6 seconds. (6 rounds)

    Regarding firearms training, the Department of Justice quarterly qualification program is superior to the annual qualification program most police departments offer. To meet DOJ standards, you must qualify four times per year and shoot 200 rounds per year. To meet police standards, you qualify once a year and shoot about 40 rounds per year. Police targets are usually larger and less demanding than DOJ targets. Most police officers would not qualify if they had to shoot the DOJ course.

    Federal agents use practical shooting skills when they qualify, but their targets have unrealistic aim points. Aim points inconsistent with tactical anatomy are unrealistic. The aim point for a headshot is a 3-inch square, and the aim point for the body is a 4x8-inch rectangle representing the center of mass. The aim point for a headshot and a heart shot should be a 5-inch circle, and the center-of-mass aim point should be replaced by the heart-shot aim point, which is in the upper chest.

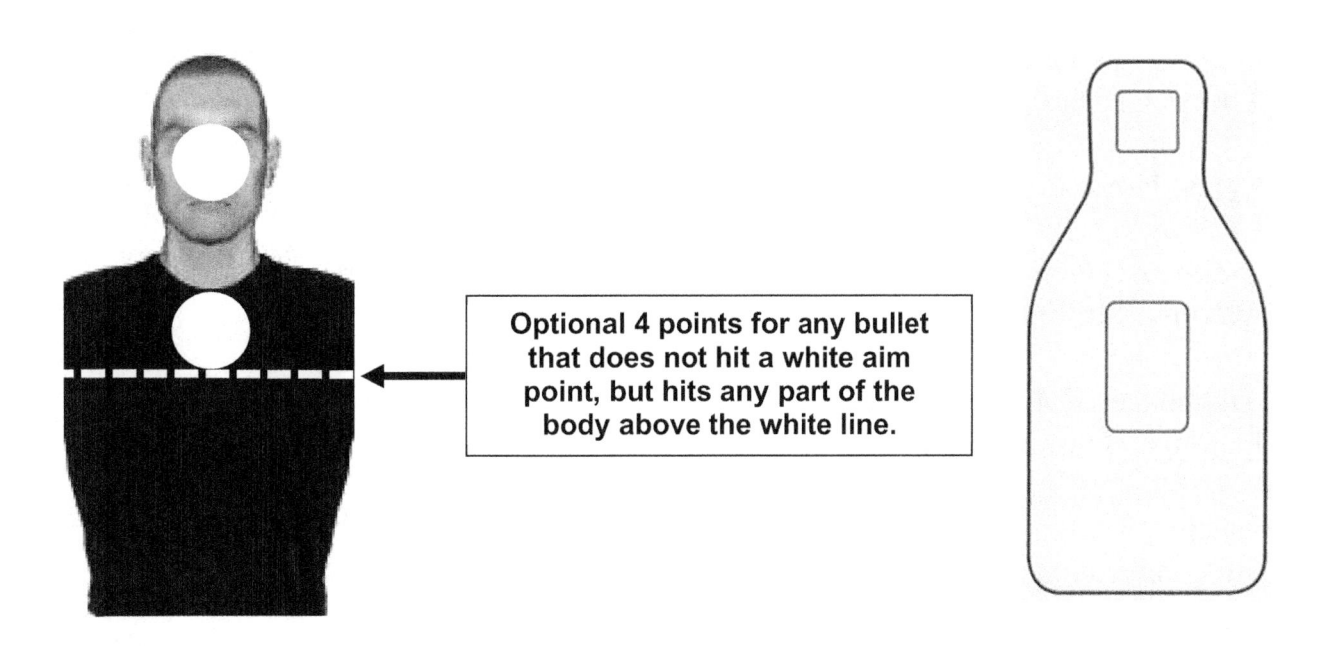

Optional 4 points for any bullet that does not hit a white aim point, but hits any part of the body above the white line.

COMBAT BIBLIOGRAPHY

Amberger, Christoph J. 1996. The secret history of the sword—adventures in ancient martial arts. Burbank, California: Unique Publications.

Anderson, James E. 1983. Grant's atlas of anatomy. 8th ed. Baltimore: Williams & Wilkins.

Anglo, Sydney. 2000. The martial arts of renaissance Europe. New Haven and London: Yale University Press.

Applegate, Rex, and Michael D. Janich. 1998. Bullseyes don't shoot back. Colorado: Paladin Press.

Applegate, Rex. 1976. Kill or get killed. Colorado: Paladin Press.

Applegate, Rex. 1993. Combat use of the double-edged fighting knife. Boulder, Colorado: Paladin Press.

Arnheim, Daniel D. 1985. Modern principles of athletic training. 6th ed. St. Louis: Times Mirror/Mosby College Publishing.

Askins, Charles. 1941. The art of handgun shooting. New York: A. S. Barnes & Company.

Askins, Charles. 1980. Askins on pistols & revolvers. Washington, D.C.: National Rifle Association.

Askins, Charles. 2007. The gunfighters. Colorado: Paladin Press.

Ayres, James Morgan. 2014. The tactical knife. New York: Skyhorse Publishing.

Backhouse, Kenneth M., and Ralph T. Hutchings. 1986. Color atlas of surface anatomy. Baltimore: Williams & Wilkins.

Backhouse, Kenneth M., and Ralph T. Hutchings. 1986. Color atlas of surface anatomy. Baltimore: Williams & Wilkins.

Baechle, Thomas R., and Roger W. Earle. eds. 2000. Essentials of strength training and conditioning. 2d ed. Champaign, Illinois: Human Kinetics.

Biddle, A. J. Drexel. 1937. Do or die. Boulder, Colorado: Paladin Press.

Blum, Lawrence. 2000. Force under pressure. New York: Lantern Books.

Bogduk, Nikolai and Lance T. Twomey. 1991. Clinical anatomy of the lumbar spine. 2d ed. Melbourne: Churchill Livingstone.

Cassidy, William L. 1993. Quick or dead. Colorado: Paladin Press.

Churchill, Robert. 1955. Churchill's shotgun book. New York: Alfred A. Knopf.

Cialdini, Robert B. 1993. Influence: the psychology of persuasion. New York: William Morrow and Company, Inc.

Clede, Bill. 1987. Police nonlethal force manual. Harrisburg, Pennsylvania: Stackpole Books.

Clemente, Carmine D. 1981. Anatomy. 2d ed. Baltimore: Urban & Schwarzenberg.

Coates Jr., James Boyd and James C. Beyer, eds. 1962. Wound ballistics. Washington D.C.: Office of Surgeon General, Department of Army.

Constance, Harry and Randall Fuerst. 1997. Good to go. New York: William Morrow & Company, Inc.

Cooper, Jeff. 1961. The complete book of modern handgunning. New York: Bramhall House.

Cooper, Jeff. 1974. Cooper on handguns. Los Angles, California: Petersen Publishing Company.

Cunningham, Eugene. 1996. Triggernometry: a gallery of gunfighters. Norman, Oklahoma: University of Oklahoma Press.

Davies, Ken. 1992. The better shot. Shropshire, England: Quiller Press.

Davis, William C. 1946. Three roads to the alamo. New York: HarperCollins.

de Beaumont, C-L. 1960. Fencing ancient art and modern sport. London: Nicholas Kaye Limited.

Di Maio, Vincent J. M. 1999. Gunshot wounds. 2d ed. Boca Raton, Florida: CRC Press.

Di Maio, Vincent J. M. 2016. Gunshot wounds. 3d ed. Boca Raton, Florida: CRC Press.

Dougherty, Paul J., ed. 2011. Gunshot wounds. Rosemont, Illinois: American Academy of Orthopaedic Surgeons.

Dressler, Joshua. 2010. Criminal law. St Paul, Minnesota: Thomson Reuters.

Enos, Brian. 1990. Practical shooting: beyond fundamentals. Clifton, Colorado: Zediker Publishing.

Fairbairn, W. E. 1942. Get tough. Boulder, Colorado: Paladin Press.

Fairbairn, W. E., and E. A. Sykes. 2008. Shooting to live. Colorado: Paladin Press.

Farnam, John S. 1997. The Farnam method of defensive shotgun and rifle shooting. Boulder, Colorado: DTI Publications.

FitzGerald, Henry J. 1930. Shooting. Colorado: Paladin Press.

Fox, Edward L., Richard W. Bowers, and Merle L. Foss. 1988. The physiological basis of physical education and athletics. Philadelphia: Saunders College Publishing.

Geller, William A., and Michael S. Scott. 1992. Deadly force. Washington, D. C.: Police Executive Research Forum.

Geller, William A., and Michael S. Scott. 1992. Deadly force. Washington, D. C.: Police Executive Research Forum.

Guyton, Arthur C., and John E. Hall. 1996. Textbook of medical physiology. 9th ed. Philadelphia: W.B. Saunders Company.

Haag, Michael G., and Lucien C. Haag. 2011. Shooting incident reconstruction. 2d ed. San Diego, California: Academic Press (Elsevier Inc.).

Hatcher, Julian. 1995. Textbook of pistols and revolvers. Fairfax, Virginia: National Rifle Association.

Hendrix, Robert C. 1972. Investigation of violent and sudden death. Springfield, Illinois: Charles C. Thomas Publisher.

Hollinshead, W. Henry and Cornelius Rosse. 1985. Textbook of anatomy. 4th ed. Philadelphia: Harper & Row, Publishers.

Hughes, Gordon, Barry Jenkins, and Robert A. 2006. Buerlein. Knives of war. Boulder, Colorado: Paladin Press.

Hutton, Alfred. 1889. Cold steel. London: William Clowes and Sons, Limited.

Jordan, Bill. 1965. No second place winner. Concord, New Hampshire: Police Bookshelf.

Kandel, Eric R., and James H. Schwartz. 1985. Principles of neural science. 2d ed. New York: Elsevier.

Kirchner, Paul. 2004. Dueling with the sword and pistol. Colorado: Paladin Press.

Kirchner, Paul. 2010. Bowie knife fights, fighters, and fighting techniques. Boulder, Colorado: Paladin Press.

Kitchner, Paul. 2009. Jim Cirillo's tales of the stakeout squad. Colorado: Paladin Press.

L'Abbat, Monsieur. 1734. The art of fencing, or, the use of the short sword. Translated by Andrew Mahon. Dublin: Dodo Press.

Lauch, Dave. 1998. The tactical 1911. Colorado: Paladin Press.

Lawrence, Eric and Mike Pannone. 2009. Tactical pistol shooting. 2d ed. Iola, Wisconsin: Krause Publications.

Leflet, David H. 2003. Motorcycle riding skills. 3d ed East Lancing, Michigan: Michigan State University.

Leflet, David H. 2005. HEMME Approach to lumbopelvic disorders. Bonifay, Florida: HEMME Approach Publications.

Levangie, Pamela K., and Cynthia C. Norkin. 2005. Joint structure & function. 4th ed. Philadelphia: F.A. Davis Company.

Levangie, Pamela K., and Cynthia C. Norkin. 2005. Joint structure & function. 4th ed. Philadelphia: F.A. Davis Company.

Loriega, James. 1999. Sevillian steel: the traditional knife-fighting arts of Spain. Boulder, Colorado: Paladin Press.

Lumley, John. S. 2008. Surface anatomy. 4th ed. Edinburgh: Churchill Livingston.

Luttgens, Kathryn and Katharine F. Wells. 1982. Kinesiology. 7th ed. Philadelphia: Saunders College Publishing.

MacPherson, Duncan. 2005. Bullet penetration. El Segundo, California: Ballistic Publications.

Madea, Burkhard, ed. 2014. Handbook of forensic medicine. New Jersey: Wiley-Blackwell.

Magill, Richard A. 2004. Motor learning and motor control. 7th ed. Boston: McGraw Hill.

Mann, Don. 2010. The modern day gunslinger. New York: Skyhorse Publishing.

McGivern, Ed. 1938. Fast and fancy revolver shooting and police training. Springfield, Massachusetts: The King-Richardson Co.

McSwain Jr., Norman E., and Morris D. Kerstein. Eds. 1987. Evaluation and management of trauma. Norwalk, Connecticut: Appleton-Century-Crofts.

Metcalf, Clyde H., ed. 1944. Marine Corps reader. New York: G.P. Putnam's Sons.

Morrison, Gregory Boyce. 1991. The modern technique of the pistol. Arizona: Gunsite Press.

Murray, Kenneth R. 2006. Training at the speed of life. Gotha, Florida: Armiger Publications, Inc.

Murray, Kenneth R. 2006. Training at the speed of light. Gotha, Florida: Armiger Publications, Inc.

Musashi, Miyamoto. 1974. The book of five rings. Translated by Victor Harris. New York: Overlook Press.

Nadi, Aldo. 1943. On fencing. Sunrise, Florida: Laureate Press.

Nadler, John. 2006. A perfect hell. New York: Presidio Press.

Norkin, Cynthia C., and D. Joyce White. 1985. Measurement of joint motion: A guide to goniometry. Philadelphia: F.A. Davis Company.

Oakeshott, R. Ewart. 1996. The archaeology of weapons. New York: Dover Publications.

Pentecost, Don, 1988. Put 'em down, take 'em out!: knife fighting techniques from Folsom Prison. Boulder, Colorado: Paladin Press.

Peterson, Harold L. 2001. Daggers and fighting knives of the western world from stone age till 1900. New York: Dover Publications.

Philips, Jim. 1986. The devil's bodyguard. New Jersey: Philips Publications.

Pinizzotto, Anthony J., Edward F. Davis, and Charles E. Miller III. 2006. Violent encounters. Clarksburg, West Virginia: United States Department of Justice, Federal Bureau of Investigation.

Plaster, John L. 1998. SOG. New York: Penguin Group (USA) Inc.

Plaxco, J. Michael. 1991. Shooting from within. Clifton, Colorado: Zediker Publishing.

Pohl, Dietmar. 2003. Tactical knives. Iola, Wisconsin: krause publications [sic].

Rasch, Philip J. 1989. Kinesiology and applied anatomy. 7th ed. Philadelphia: Lea & Febiger.

Richard, Colin. 2007. Fiore dei Libera 1409. Germany: Arts of Mars Books.

Rosa, Joseph G. 1969. The gunfighter: man or myth?. Norman, Oklahoma: University of Oklahoma Press.

Rutledge, Devallis. 1988. The officer survival manual. Placerville, California: Custom Publishing Company.

Salomon, Dustin, 2016. Building shooters. Silver Point, Tennessee: Innovative Services and Solutions, LLC.

Samaha, Joel. 2008. Criminal law. 9th ed. Belmont, California: Thomas Learning, Inc.

Saurez, Gabriel. 1996. The tactical shotgun. Boulder, Colorado: Paladin Press.

Schultz, Duane. 2014. Evans Carlson, marine raider. Yardley, Pennsylvania: Westholme Publishing, LLC.

Sifakis, Carl. 1991. Encyclopedia of assassinations. New York: Facts On File.

Smith, George W. 2001. Carlson's raid—the daring marine assault on Makin. Novato, California: Presidio Press, Inc.

Snyder, LeMoyne. 1967. Homicide investigation. 2d ed. Springfield, Illinois: Charles C. Thomas Publisher.

Spitz, Werner U., and Daniel J. Spitz, eds. 2006. Spitz and Fisher's medicolegal investigation of death. 4th ed. Springfield, Illinois: Charles. C. Thomas Publisher, LTD.

Springer, Joseph A. 2001. The black devil brigade. Pacifica, California: Pacifica Military History.

Styers, John. 1974. Cold steel. Boulder, Colorado: Paladin Press.

Swan, Kenneth G., and Roy C. Swan. 1989. Gunshot wounds pathophysiology and management. 2d ed. Chicago: Year Book Medical Publishers, Inc.

Talhoffer, Hans. 2000, Medieval combat. Translated by Mark Rector. Great Britain: Greenhill Books, Lionel Leventhal Limited.

Taubert, Robert k. 2012. Rattenkrieg!. North Reading, Massachusetts: Saber Press.

Taylor, Chuck. 1985. The combat shotgun and submachine gun. Boulder, Colorado: Paladin Press.

Taylor, John. 2003. Shotshells & ballistics. Long Beach, California: Safari Press, Inc.

Tedeschi, Marc. 2003. The Art of the Weapon. Connecticut: Weatherhill.

Thompson, Leroy. 2011. Fairbairn-Sykes commando dagger. Great Britain: Osprey Publishing, Ltd.

Trachtman, Paul. 1974. The gunfighters. Alexandria, Virginia: Time-Life Books.

Tzu, Sun. 1988. The art of war. Translated by Thomas Cleary. London: Shambhala.

U.S. Marine Corps. 1996. U.S. Marines close-quarters manual. Boulder, Colorado: Paladin Press.

Vail, Jason. 2006. Medieval and renaissance dagger combat. Boulder, Colorado: Paladin Press.

Vilos, Mitch and Evan Vilos. 2010. Self-defense laws of all 50 states. Centerville, Utah: Guns West Publishing, Inc.

Vistica, Gregory L. 2003. The education of Lieutenant Kerrey. New York: St. Martin's Press.

Warlow, Tom. 2012. Firearms, the law, and forensic ballistics. 3d ed. Boca Raton, Florida: CRC Press.

Waterson, James. 2008. The Ismaili assassins a history of medieval murder. London: Frontline Books.

Wiener, Stanley L., and John Barrett. 1986. Trauma management for civilian and military physicians. Philadelphia: W. B. Saunders Company.

Williams, James S. 2006. Tactical anatomy instructor manual. Big Lake, Texas: Tactical Anatomy Systems, LLC.

Williams, Peter L., and Roger Warwick. 1980. Gray's anatomy. 36th ed. Philadelphia: W.B. Saunders.

Windsor, Guy. 2012. The Medieval Dagger—Mastering the art of arms. Wheaton, Illinois: FreeLance Academy Press.

Zabinski, Grzegorz. 2002. Codex Wallerstein—a medieval fighting book from the fifteenth century on longsword, falchion, dagger, and wrestling. Boulder, Colorado: Paladin Press.

Essay dated 1875 (New York)

Author unknown. Jeff Cooper, forward. 2004. The pistol as a weapon of defense in the house and on the road. Colorado: Paladin Press.

DVDs

Applegate, Rex. 1995. Point shooting. Boulder, Colorado: Paladin Press.

Cirillo, Jim. 1996. Modern-day gunfighter. Boulder, Colorado: Paladin Press.

Fackler, Martin and Jason Alexander. 2006. Deadly effects. Boulder, Colorado: Paladin Press.

Grover, Jim. 2002. Combative pistol. Boulder, Colorado: Paladin Press.

Jordan, Bill. 1989. Fast and fancy shooting. Boulder, Colorado: Paladin Press.

Focus on the tactical handgun skills that are most likely to save your life. Based on FBI statistics, shooting targets 50 yards away or decreasing the speed of your draw or the time it takes to reload by a fraction of a second will not save your life. What will save your life is being able to make a headshot or heart shot at distances between 75 feet and the end of your barrel. A contact shot to the head with a blank cartridge can be fatal. When target shooters look at a target, they see a target that will not shoot back. When tactical shooters look at a target, they see a target that might shoot back. It's hard to say which is worse: practicing shooting skills that have no tactical value or not practicing tactical shooting skills enough to be combat effective when facing a deadly threat.

ABOUT THE AUTHORS

Dave Leflet has a master of science degree from Michigan State University, where he majored in security and criminal investigation. After graduation, he joined the Miami-Dade Police Department. He was a Hostage Release Team sniper, a Special Response Team squad leader, and a state-certified defensive tactics instructor. He received a 3rd-degree black belt in Juai Kung Karbo from Bert Rodriquez and a 5th-degree black belt in Karate from Leo Thalassites, who was a police defensive tactics instructor and a member of the World's Martial Arts Hall of Fame. Dave shot distinguished expert with revolvers and 1911 pistols.

Dave executed hundreds of break orders that authorized a forcible entry and faced dozens of deadly confrontations involving knives or guns. He performed about a dozen empty-hand knife or gun disarms and participated in one knife fight. The courses Dave created and taught included personal injury reduction training, emergency first aid, and counterterrorism. He also wrote computer-based training programs for law enforcement.

Curtis Porter was a U.S. Marine who served during the Gulf War. When stationed in Kuwait, he was a sergeant in charge of a Marine Reaper Unit. Curtis received medals and commendations for devotion to duty, courage under fire, and uncommon valor during combat operations.

During the Gulf War, Curtis developed handgun techniques that later evolved into the Porter Method. These techniques resulted from using a handgun as his primary weapon when conducting numerous building searches. He refined these techniques when serving as a Marine small-arms instructor. After leaving the Corps, Curtis worked as a police officer and a member of the DEA Drug Taskforce. Unlike most police departments, Curtis teaches tactical shooting instead of target shooting. He has trained elite military units, correction officers, police officers, and federal agents, and he is a state-certified police firearms instructor and a gunsmith.

> **A Steel Challenge Grandmaster named Ken Verderame stated that you should pay attention to any shooting expert's pedigree—and we agree. If you want to be a competitive target shooter, listen to someone who has target shooting expertise. On the other hand, if you want to be a tactical shooter, you listen to someone who has repeatedly used a handgun or shotgun for self-defense and survived.**

Printed in Great Britain
by Amazon